Her Mistletoe Cowboy

Big Sky Christmas, Book 3

Jenna Hendricks

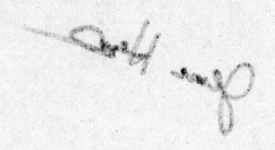

Books by Jenna Hendricks

See these titles and more: https://JennaHendricks.com

Other Books by J.L. Hendricks (my 1st pen name)

Book 1: Coming soon

<u>Chronicles of the Fae Princess</u> –

Trilogy Published by LMBPN Publishing

See these titles and get their links at
https://www.jlhendricksauthor.com/

Newsletter Sign-up

B y signing up for my newsletter, you will get a free copy of the prequel to the Triple J Ranch series, Finding Love in Montana. As well as more free stories!

If you want to make sure you hear about the latest and greatest, sign up for my newsletter at: Subscribe to Jenna Hendricks' newsletter. I will only send out a few e-mails a month. I'll do cover reveals, snippets of new books, and giveaways or promos in the newsletter, some of which will only be available to newsletter subscribers. https://jennahendricks.com/newsletter/

Contents

Chapter 1

Cody Makinaw had always loved the first snow of the year…when he was a boy. Now that he was a man, it only infuriated him when it came early. And this year, it was extra early.

"For Pete's sake." Cody pursed his lips and shook his head. "Why does everything have to happen at once?" He wasn't speaking to anyone in particular; he was all alone, filling the gas tank on his old, beat-up Ford F250 that had seen better days. Just last week the odometer had tripped the three-hundred-thousand mark. Thankfully, these old tanks were built to last.

"Hey, cowboy. Have you tried the latest creation from the McKinley farm?" Lisa Hamilton, manager of the Sip 'n' Go, handed Cody a pastry.

Cody furrowed his brows. "What's this?" He took the offered pastry in his free hand and sniffed it. "A scone with fruit? No thanks. I'm not really the teatime sort of man."

Lisa giggled. "No, silly. It's not that sort of scone." She tilted her head. "Well, maybe. But it's not very sweet if that's what you're worried about. It's really good. It's a homemade huckleberry scone. We've recently started selling them here." She waved to the convenience store attached to the gas station.

With a frown, Cody took a bite and blinked. Then he took another bite. After he swallowed both bites, his frown loosened and he nodded. "Not bad. Huckleberry? These must be expensive."

Lisa shook her head. "Not so much. And the first one is on me." She looked up at the light flurries drifting down. It wasn't quite cold enough for the flakes to stick, but she caught a few on her palm and watched as the little bits of ice slowly melted in her hand. "Looks like we might be in for a lot of snow this year."

He grunted. "I hate when it snows before Halloween. Makes the final trimming of my trees more difficult and slow-going."

"Will you open the Christmas tree farm early this year?" Lisa wiped the melted signs of an early winter on her thigh and grinned. "I love it when there's a lot of snow and you bring out the sleigh."

Cody owned and ran Frenchtown's only Christmas tree farm. He grunted and looked up. The surrounding mountains were still green, as the snow wasn't even sticking yet on the local mountain range. "We'll see. It's too early to tell. If we get a good storm and it sticks, I'll open up the first weekend of November." He turned back to look at her. "Do you have enough of these scones for me to take back to the boys?"

Lisa's grin ran from ear to ear. "I'll go and pack you up a dozen. Come on in when you've filled up your tanks."

"Thanks." Cody went back to checking the progress on his tank. The truck had an extra tank in the bed that he used to fill up the equipment around his ranch.

When he got home, he brought in the box of scones and headed to the kitchen. "Grandpops, you home?" Cody looked in the kitchen and discovered his grandfather snoozing in a rocker close to the wood stove used to heat the mudroom and dining room.

Hoping to not wake his grandfather, Cody silently set the box of treats on the counter and turned to leave.

"Huh?" The old man snorted and jerked in his rocker. "I wasn't sleeping."

Trying to keep from laughing, Cody coughed and shook his head. "Of course not." He walked back to the counter, took out one of the tasty treats, and put it on a napkin before handing it to his grandpops. "I got these from the Sip 'n' Go this morning. Turns out the McKinleys had a bumper crop of huckleberries this year and they're now selling these out at the gas station."

"Scones?" Grandpops scrunched his nose and gave the offered treat back to Cody. "I'm not a tea-and-biscuits sort of man. Give me a good, strong cup of black coffee and a pie any day. Now if you'd brought me back a huckleberry pie, I wouldn't have turned that down." He grinned, revealing a mouth missing the top row of teeth.

"Grandpops"—Cody sighed—"where are your dentures? You know you can't go around toothless. It gives people the creeps." He took the scone back, knowing his grandfather couldn't eat anything other than mushed peas or mashed potatoes, anyway. "Go get your teeth in, then come back and try this. It's really good."

The old man grumbled. "I don't need no teeth, and I don't need no ladies' sweet treat. When your grandma passed, God rest her soul, I stopped eating sweet treats."

"And you started eating candy bars instead." Cody pointed to his grandpops. "Which is what caused your teeth to rot and fall out." Not that he was any better, but he kept it to one candy bar instead of four or five a day like his grandfather had done.

Grandpops grumbled.

"I can't understand you without your teeth. Go put them in and then we can get going outside. It's already starting to snow. Nothing has stuck yet, but you know what this means." Cody put the treat back in the box and put on a fresh pot of coffee. Knowing his grandpops the way he did, they'd need a new pot to fill up their thermoses before heading out into the cold and blustery day.

Cody also put a few of the tasty treats into a bag to take to the farm hands. They'd be ready for a treat, especially with this cold front moving through. They always needed to eat more when it snowed. The extra energy would help them get through a long day of trimming and measuring the Christmas trees.

It had nothing to do with him wanting another scone. No siree, he wasn't trying to justify eating more of those deliciously crumbly homemade scones made with fresh huckleberries. If only they had huckleberry bushes on their property.

Instead, they had too many trees these days, and a handful of maple trees used specifically for growing mistletoe, since the kissing-bough type of mistletoe wasn't native to Montana. Cody's great-great-grandfather put in the maple trees ages ago to grow the only Christmas mistletoe in the state. Now, in addition to selling Christmas trees they also sold mistletoe boughs, though that didn't make them much money.

In fact, Cody figured it cost more to grow and harvest than they were making in profits these days. When he had suggested they stop messing with the mistletoe, his grandpops just about had a coronary. So for now, they still sold the kissing plant.

Not that he'd received a kiss under the mistletoe since high school. But the locals and his few remaining clients all liked the romantic parasite.

"Alright Grandpops, let's saddle up and head out to the back of the fields, where the boys are trimming the trees." Cody put his bag of treats into a saddlebag and helped his grandfather get their horses ready.

His grandfather grinned and showed off his pearly white dentures that didn't quite match his lower teeth.

Cody looked to heaven and shook his head. "Why me, Lord?"

They only had a couple of weeks left before they had to start delivering orders. Sadly, Cody had lost a few contracts over the past few years and they had fewer and fewer orders to fill each year. The "green" movement in the US had really hurt his tree sales. People thought that buying plastic trees—which produced more harmful chemical emissions than cutting down a real tree—was better for the environment, but it wasn't. Sure, those fake trees were getting more and more real looking. But they weren't nearly as beautiful as a proper spruce or a noble fir. Not to mention, the artificial tree smells never were the same and didn't last as long as the real tree, when you took proper care of it.

If Cody didn't find a way to drum up more business and soon, he'd lose his farm.

Chapter 2

L isa Hamilton called the McKinley ranch to let them know how well the scones had done. "Sadie, we've sold out of the scones today. Can I double my order?"

"Really? Already? But you've only had them for a few hours." Sadie McKinley, daughter of Boone and Silvia McKinley, the owners of the McKinley ranch a few miles outside of Frenchtown, grinned.

Sadie was a marketing manager before she was laid off last year at her big marketing firm in Seattle, Washington. After an unsuccessful attempt at finding a new job, she went home to help her parents while she tried to figure out what she wanted to do with her life.

"Yup, I offered free scones to a few people who ended up buying me out after they tried them. I think you might be giving Lottie a run for her money this year." Lisa chuckled and waved as a regular customer walked into the store.

"Compete with the Frenchtown Roasting Company? Are you crazy? Lottie's creations are the best. Her coffee and pastries are better than anything I ever had in Seattle. That was probably one of the things I missed the most every time I went back to Seattle." Sadie had only come to town to visit a few times since Lottie opened up her shop, but every visit she picked up at least ten pounds of coffee to bring home, and wished she could also bring the entire pastry cabinet back with her. Especially after her Christmas visits.

The one thing Sadie wanted most were the gingerbread lattes that didn't show up on the menu until Thanksgiving. Since coming home this past spring, she'd bugged Lottie on multiple occasions to serve that drink again. But the coffee shop owner and barista was adamant about not starting the Christmas treats until Thanksgiving.

Lisa chuckled. "I don't think we'll be competing, but I do think your huckleberry scones will bring in a few more people than usual. Oh, also, do you know Cody Makinaw?"

"Cody? Isn't he the guy who owns the Christmas tree farm?" Sadie remembered him from around town and back in school. But Cody was three years older than her thirty-two, if she was thinking of the same guy.

"Yes, he is. He was here earlier today and bought a dozen to bring back to the farm. He might be calling you to order some. He thought they were divine."

"Cody, the guy who never smiles or even talks to anyone, said the word '*divine*'?" Sadie wouldn't believe that one.

"Well, he may not have said divine, but if his almost-smile was anything to go on, then yeah. He really enjoyed them." Lisa wasn't exactly exaggerating, but the man had grunted and kept eating his scone while they'd spoken. Then came in to get a dozen.

"Why would he be calling me? If he wants more, shouldn't he just get them from you?" Her dry throat brought Sadie over to the coffee pot, where she poured herself another cup of hot joe.

"Because he wants to buy in bulk. I think he's planning on selling them at the Christmas tree farm."

Sadie considered the idea for a moment and smiled. "I think we could help him. I froze way too many berries this year. I should have sold off more buckets, but just didn't have the time to reach out to more people." Their farm normally produced about a hundred gallons of huckleberries, give or take a few. But this year, it was almost three times as many. Getting them all harvested had taken a long time. They did have a few local customers who bought all of their surplus in a normal year, but they weren't interested in tripling their orders this year.

"I gave him your number, just in case." Lisa looked around to make sure no one was listening in. "I think he might need to make some extra cash this year. I heard his farm wasn't doing too well."

While Sadie hated gossip, she couldn't resist asking, "What do you mean? I thought Christmas tree farms were cash cows."

"Not lately. With the pretty fake trees, and the ability to re-use them for several years, a lot of people think they're a better use of money. Some even think they're better for the environment." Lisa had never used a fake tree for her house, but with the local fire codes, she did use one for the Sip 'n' Go's Christmas display.

"But real trees are so pretty and smell so much better than those chemicals. And we always turn our tree into mulch when we take it down." Sadie thought back to when she lived in the city. "And when I was in Seattle, the trash trucks came by after Christmas and picked up the trees. They'd make wood chips for the city parks. Although, it was a real pain to lug a tree up into my apartment every year. We didn't have a big elevator, so I had to carry it up four flights of stairs. It wasn't easy."

"I think that the media gets on a subject and forgets to fact-check. Just like the debacle with the plastic straws." As manager of the Sip 'n' Go, Lisa was angry that the plastic straw issue had gone the way it did. It was stupid, really. The other options were plastic lids you could drink out of, still using plastic. And the paper straws were a joke. She refused to swap out the plastic straws.

"True. If people would just do a little investigating on their own, they'd find out a lot of what the media tells us is just plain wrong. Most organizations who own media outlets have their own agendas to push, or products they want to sell more of." As a marketing manager, Sadie knew firsthand what these companies were really about.

Her beliefs were part of why she was laid off when her company had to make cuts. During a company meeting, she had once spoken up against one of their clients and their not-so-altruistic motives behind a particular campaign she was working on. Her boss moved her to a different project, thankfully, but someone up high must have remembered the stink she'd caused and her name ended up on the list of people to cut. She wasn't the only one to lose her job when the company lost a few larger clients.

Which was why she had been taking on small marketing jobs here and there. Until Sadie knew exactly what she wanted, she had started up her own tiny marketing company. She even wooed away one of her old clients, who'd been none too happy with her replacement. It wasn't enough work to support herself, but it was enough to keep making her car and insurance payments as well as decent pocket money.

"Thanks for the referral, Lisa. I think this might be a great way to use up our extra huckleberries, and maybe I can even make a few pies to sell them. If I remember correctly, old man Makinaw loves a good pie." Sadie had seen Cody's grandfather eating pie in Lottie's shop quite a few times since she'd returned home. There were other people around town who loved huckleberry pie as well.

With a chuckle and a promise to sell more, Lisa said goodbye and hung up.

Sadie sat there considering how many huckleberries she'd need if she was going to supply the tree farm with scones and more for the next two months. Then she went to her mother and asked if she still had Grandma's old cookbook with huckleberry recipes. Her grandma used to make the best huckleberry taffy.

Although, pulling taffy was a lot of work. Maybe she wouldn't suggest selling huckleberry taffy at the tree farm.

The next day she did, in fact, receive a call from Cody. Much to her surprise, he remembered her.

"Sadie, how ya been? It's been a while." Cody Makinaw wasn't very good at making small talk.

"Hiya, Cody. What can I do for you today?" Sadie knew what he wanted, but she wasn't about to let him know she knew what he wanted.

"I had one of your scones at the gas station the other day and it was really good. In fact, even my grandpops said it wasn't half bad."

"Not half bad? Thanks, I think." Sarcasm dripped from her voice. It didn't sound as though the Makinaw family was all that interested in her scones.

"That's a compliment. I don't think he's had a scone in over twenty years."

Cody did sound contrite, and she didn't want to give him a hard time. Since they really weren't friends, and barely even acquaintances, she decided to take the strange words as a compliment. "Thank you, I appreciate the kind words. If you're interested in more, we're making a larger batch for the Sip 'n' Go tomorrow."

"Actually, I was hoping I could place a larger order for the tree farm, once we open the store. I was going to make coffee and cocoa for the guests, and think it might be nice to sell some treats as well. And huckleberry treats are the specialty of the area."

"How large an order? We don't have commercial ovens or anything like that, so I'm not sure how many we could make a day." She hadn't really considered yet how many batches she could whip up on her own each day. She did have a couple of projects she was working on for clients. The holiday campaigns were all done, but two of her clients wanted to do something extra-special for Valentine's Day, so she had to work on those now and get them done and finished before Thanksgiving. Especially if she wanted to take the entire month of December off to enjoy the Christmas season.

A scratching sound came over the phone line, and just as she was about to ask if he was still there, Cody said a number. She gasped. "Every day? You need that many each day for the entire time you're open?"

"I don't know about that. But we're hoping to attract a lot of people this year. We're going to add sleigh rides for a fee, photos with Santa, and I was thinking about bringing in a few rides and games. I think if we can make it more like a carnival atmosphere, we'll get more customers from the surrounding areas." It was all stated matter-of-factly, but Sadie could hear the trepidation in Cody's voice.

"Well, what sort of marketing do you have set up?" Without a good campaign, Sadie knew he wouldn't get anyone outside of their town and maybe a handful of families from Missoula if he ran an ad of some sort.

"Marketing?" This time confusion and fear laced Cody's words.

Sadie knew he was in way over his head. Something inside of her said to help the poor cowboy. While she didn't know him well, he was a neighbor. And wasn't it her Christian duty to help out a neighbor? It certainly was part of the cowboy/cowgirl code.

Growing up out in the wilds of Montana—well, okay maybe not the wilds. But she did grow up in a very small town. It was instilled in all ranchers and farmers to help their neighbors, so from a very young age Sadie had been trained to help out where she could.

Her family owned and operated a farm outside of Frenchtown, Montana. They raised pigs, a few cattle, and plenty of vegetables for their family, as well as enough to sell at market. They even had a few cows for milk, and a few goats as well. Most people would call her family – pig farmers. It held a negative connotation, but once bacon was in play, people forgot all about the pigsties she grew up around.

Goat milk wasn't her thing, but there were plenty of neighbors who liked it. It was also good for cats and dogs. In fact, their barn cats were given weekly treats of the thick white drink. They always employed a feisty bunch of cats to ensure the mouse population in their barns and outbuildings was as close to zero as possible.

Raising pigs like they did tended to attract mice and even rats. They always had slop in the pigsties, which was basically leftover food from their own table. Scraps always attracted vermin. Barn cats were always needed on ranches and farms.

Getting her mind back on the conversation at hand, she went on to educate the confused cowboy. "Without a good marketing plan, you won't be able to attract enough customers to afford the outlay you're talking about. If you're going to set up new attractions and booths that you didn't have before, you'll need to invest money to get those items. Even if you're planning on building the booths from scratch."

"I see." Cody paused. "How do I go about putting together a marketing plan? Is it expensive?"

"You're in luck. I just happen to be an excellent marketing manager with a small business of my own. I'd be happy to help you promote your Christmas tree farm and all of the events you're planning."

"Whoa, I don't think I can afford much."

"Why don't we do some sort of trade?" Knowing that most cowboys had their pride to consider, Sadie knew she couldn't just offer to help him for free. She'd have to accept something from him in exchange for her services. And after what Lisa had said, she wasn't going to let the only Christmas tree farm in their region go out of business.

"I don't know what I have that you could use." Cody seemed to hesitate, then added, "But I could definitely give you your pick of as many trees and mistletoe as you want. We're going to have a lot of extra trees this year."

"I never did like a fake tree." Sadie licked her lips and considered that they could get a giant tree this year for their entryway. The front of the house had large, picturesque windows almost twenty feet high. They had a wonderful view of the surrounding mountains out the front of their house. They'd never been able to afford a tree that tall so they only put one in the family room, in the back of the house.

One year, she went looking at the giant trees in Seattle and found out they cost anywhere from three hundred to five hundred dollars, depending on the type and height. And after Christmas her parents would donate their tree to the local 4H club so they could turn it into mulch, or chips, since they didn't have the equipment to mulch it themselves. But a Christmas tree farm most certainly had that sort of equipment.

In the spring, they would have to buy bags and bags of mulch. She could probably get Cody to take the trees back and turn them into mulch for their own needs this year. Her parents would still need to buy more, but with two trees, one of which would be at least fifteen feet tall, they'd have a decent start.

"Well, if you want to come out this week and see what we've got planned, I'm sure we could come to some sort of agreement," Cody said. "And I still want to discuss buying your scones. Do you also make huckleberry pies? My grandpops loves a good huckleberry pie. In fact, it's his favorite."

Huckleberry pies? Sadie could make a fantastic huckleberry pie if she could find her grandmother's recipe. While she didn't want to use up all her frozen berries over the next two months, she did want to use the vast majority of them. They'd need the freezer space when it came time to butcher a few pigs. Which they normally did in January. And she had a few ideas in addition to what Cody wanted to do.

"Yes, I'd love to come out and see the farm. I'll bring over some more scones and a pie when I come out. How about Friday? Will that work?" She'd also prepare a small presentation with a few ideas.

"Sounds good. What time did you want to meet?"

When they'd set up a time to meet and said goodbye, Sadie grinned and rubbed her hands together. She was going to have a lot of fun with this project. She only hoped that Cody would agree to what she wanted to do.

Chapter 3

When Friday afternoon arrived, Cody felt sweat forming on his forehead. It wasn't hot outside—in fact, it had snowed again overnight. This time there were still flakes covering the ground. It wasn't a lot, just enough to tease the upcoming winter season. He also felt like he'd swallowed a lead brick.

It wasn't as though this was a date. His nervousness had nothing to do with a woman coming over and everything to do with Sadie McKinley and the fact that she might be able to help his farm recover. He had no desire to be the Makinaw who lost the family farm. He was the fifth generation to work this land, and he'd be tarred and feathered before he let it slip away.

Just last night he'd had a difficult conversation with his grandpops.

"Son"—Joseph Makinaw put a hand on Cody's shoulder after dinner—"we need to talk about the finances of this here ranch."

That was the first time he begun sweating since the warm summer ended and the cold fall weather dropped in like a lead weight. Cody's head dropped, and he sighed. "Yes, I know. But I've got plans, Grandpops. In fact, tomorrow a lady's coming over to help me with a marketing plan."

Joseph chuckled. "Cody, my boy, it's going to take more than a good marketing campaign, which you can't afford, to turn things around."

"You know I've got more plans for this year. I've already spoken to a few small carnival operators. I found one who has a few rides and games they can bring in. They'll even give us a percentage of the profits." Cody was pretty proud of himself for that idea. He knew it wouldn't make a lot of money, but it would help. And every penny counted.

After the old man took a seat, he looked into his grandson's eyes. "It's going to take a lot more than a few extra dollars this year. We need plans for the future as well. Maybe even another source of income to keep things going. Real trees just aren't in demand like they used to be."

Cody nodded, knowing his grandfather was right. They needed to diversify. "Maybe we can start running cattle. I've heard of a few new trends, like cow cuddling. And the elites in some big cities are talking about how healthy the meat from Scottish Highland cows is. I thought we might want to raise them. We could be the first cattle ranch in this state to offer Highland cows to a new market."

"That's all fine and good, but where are you going to get the capital to start a new venture? It takes several hundred head of cattle, not to mention at least one bull, to start a new cattle ranch." Joseph took a drink of his coffee. They liked to sit around the kitchen table after dinner and discuss the business of the farm as well as the next day's activities. And decaf coffee was always on the table, along with a sweet treat.

"I know. That's why I was thinking about what to do to raise more money this Christmas season. Sadie said she could help put together a marketing plan. Get the word out about the new attractions here this year. Maybe we could even raise the prices on the trees and put out a coupon. You know, make people think they're getting a good deal." Cody wasn't sure about this option, but it was something he'd thought about this week. He'd have to ask Sadie what she thought about it.

They hadn't raised prices on the trees in quite a while, and he knew that other tree farms had raised their prices on customers. He should be able to add a few dollars to each one they sold onsite and still be cheaper than the lots in the big cities. That was one of the benefits of going to a Christmas tree farm: lower prices, since there wasn't any need to pay for transport or a middleman. Buying direct was always the best way to go.

Now that the time had come, Cody was nervous. He had too much riding on this Christmas to mess this up. All night he kept going over what he and his grandpops had discussed—and the way his grandfather moved. The old man wasn't getting any younger.

When the doorbell rang, Cody stood up from the kitchen table where he had been drinking coffee. His grandpops was out back with the hands working the trees. Sadly, his grandfather got older and frailer every year. Cody didn't think the old man would be helping outside for too many more Christmases. He'd have to find something for his grandpops to do while staying inside more. The cold weather couldn't be good for an old bag of bones. Especially when said old man had such bad arthritis he had to take prescription medication for it.

Cody opened the front door to a pretty cowgirl. He hadn't remembered Sadie being beautiful, and the woman standing on his front porch would be considered beautiful by any man with eyes. She was about average height for a woman, and she had dirty blond hair hanging in waves down her back and over her shoulders. But what really caught his attention were her sparkling green eyes. They reminded him of brilliant gems.

"Sadie?" he asked.

When the woman smiled in return and nodded her head, it was like looking at the brilliance of fireworks. Her face sparkled as the sun shone on her profile, and his breath caught in his throat.

"Yes, it's nice to see you again, Cody. You don't look as though you've changed much since high school." She put her hand out to shake.

When Cody took it, his breathing went back to normal and he tried to smile, but his mouth wouldn't work. After a long pause, his manners kicked in and he opened the door. "Please, come in." Once he had closed the door, he took her coat and hat.

"I don't think I've been out here since I was a kid. I remember when my parents used to take us all here every year to get a tree. It was such a wonderful experience. My dad always cut the tree himself after us kids fought over who got to choose it." Sadie chuckled and followed Cody to the kitchen.

"Would you like a cup of coffee?" He motioned for her take a seat at the table. "I think most of the kids in the area fight over who gets to choose a tree. It's just one of those rights of passage." Growing up, Cody had always envied the families who came to the farm. Even the fighting made him wish he had a sibling. But sadly, his parents only had him.

"Yes, please. With cream and sugar." Sadie took a seat and looked out the back window at the barn. Just behind it were rows and rows of the various Christmas trees this farm was known for. She grinned and thanked Cody when he put a cup of hot coffee in front of her.

Cody went to the fridge, pulled out a container of real cream, and set it on the table next to the sugar bowl. "Please, help yourself. I also have some goat's milk if you prefer that for your coffee."

"No, cow's cream will be perfect. Thanks." She grinned and set to work making her coffee just the way she liked.

After she took two sips, Sadie looked up at Cody. "How about we take a tour of the grounds and you show me what you have planned for this year? Then we can come back and set to work planning on how best to get the word out about your farm and the events."

"Perfect. Would you like an insulated coffee mug to take your drink with you?" He pointed to her mostly full cup of coffee.

"That'd be great, thanks. It's really cold out there today. And the snow from last night didn't melt yet, like the previous two snowfalls did." Taking her cup in her hands, Sadie poured the remains into the lidded mug Cody offered her.

As they walked to the barn, Cody pointed out the signpost listing the various types of trees they offered.

Sadie read it over and looked at the pictures. Then she pointed. "The noble fir is my favorite type of tree."

Cody tilted his head and looked at Sadie. She was glowing, a smile covering her entire face. "Why the noble?" He had an idea, but he always thought it best to ask the customer why they wanted a particular tree.

"Because the branches are strong. The scent screams Christmas, and I like the gaps between the branches. It makes it easier to hang our large, heavy ornaments."

"I see. And do you make your own ornaments?" Cody asked.

She nodded. "Of course we do. We also have some store-bought ones. But my favorite are those we make as a family. Sometimes we get together on a night with bad weather and Mom will make up a batch of gingerbread that's designed for ornaments, not cookies." Sadie giggled. "And we have a family fun night where we all make and decorate our own ornaments to add to the tree."

"Do you ever do the ornament decorating in town?" Cody had been to the town's various Christmas events over the years, but since he took over operations of the family farm, he usually didn't have the energy to go into town after a long day of selling trees.

With a nod and a gleam in her eye, Sadie told Cody about her favorite ornament. "One year when I was in high school, we made these tiny gingerbread houses. This was back before the full-size gingerbread house competitions at the coffee shop. My ornament was about the size of my hand." She held out her hand to show him the approximate size. "We could choose from three different sizes, and mine was the largest at the time."

When Sadie looked off into the distance, Cody came up with an idea. "What if we had our own ornament-decorating station? Do you think people would like to make more than one ornament each year with their family?"

Sadie's eyes widened and her mouth formed an O. "Yes, I think they would. Not everyone can make the one night each year in town that we do the ornament decorating. And besides, if you had it here every day while your lot was open, then I know you'd get families coming together and spending quality time with their loved ones. It's really a great idea." Then she frowned.

"What? Is something wrong?" Just a moment ago she'd seemed excited by the idea. Now Cody wondered what could have caused her to look worried.

Sadie waved a hand in front of her face. "No, no. Nothing's wrong. Just thinking logistics. You'd have to have a lot of dough premade and already cooked, just waiting for people to buy and decorate. That's a lot of work."

Cody scratched the little scruff on his chin. "I see what you mean. Is there another way we could do ornament-making? Does it have to be with cookie dough?"

She shook her head. "Not necessarily. You could cut out designs in wood if you have the time and equipment."

Sadie jumped when Cody slapped his hand on his thigh. "Well, I'll be. This will be a great way to kill two birds."

"How so?" Sadie asked.

"I needed to find something indoors that my grandfather could do. Working outside in this cold weather is wreaking havoc on his joints."

"And he's good with wood?"

Cody nodded. "Yes, he is. And he has all sorts of equipment for cutting small pieces into various shapes. He can also take small branches and slice them to make them a flat circle. We have wood-burning kits that the men can use to etch in designs."

"We could also offer up premade designs in vinyl to put on the wood discs." Sadie began rattling off all sorts of options, including making the most delicate of DIY ornaments, the blown egg.

The two spent the next few minutes writing down more ideas for the decorating station they were going to set up. Then Sadie's head popped up from her note-taking. "What about wreaths? Do you use the clippings from the trees to make real wreaths?"

Cody thought about it a moment. "We used to. My mom used to operate a little area close to the store where people could buy the materials they needed to create their own customs wreaths. But we haven't done that in a long time."

"It would take someone working that booth who knew exactly what they were doing so they could help the customers. But I bet we could find a few older ladies who'd love a chance to work the booth." Sadie already had a few in mind.

Cody blew out a long breath. "I don't know about hiring people. It just might cost me more than I'll make this year."

"It's possible," Sadie agreed. "But I think if we can get a good set of activities going, I can set up a marketing plan that will help you make a lot more than what you're spending."

"Let's continue the tour and discuss ideas. When we're done, we can write it all down and go from there." Cody wanted to do more, but he had so little to work with, he wasn't sure what he could afford. However, if some of these ideas would help keep his grandfather out of the cold, then he'd do whatever he could to find a good plan to keep his grandpops warm this winter.

"What about raising the prices of the trees and then offering coupons to the locals?" It was a thought Cody had been chewing on for a while now, but still wasn't sure it would work.

"Why, I think that's a great idea, Cody. Only your regular customers will know that you've raised your prices. And you won't be the first to do so. Most tree farms raised prices over the past few years." Sadie had done some homework on trees and pricing in preparation for this meeting. She had actually wanted to bring up the price sheet herself but hadn't had a chance yet.

As he walked Sadie around the tree farm, he guided her away from any debris on the ground. He'd have to talk to his guys about cleaning up the pathways. People needed safe walking areas if he was going to have a herd of customers here this year. The last thing he needed…

Before he could finish his thought, Sadie bumped into him. "Oomph. Sorry about that." Sadie had put her hand on his arm, and Cody took her by her elbow to keep her from falling.

She teetered for a moment, then stood up straight and looked behind her. "There's a hole or depression or something under the snow we just walked over."

Cody went back and forth between wanting to hold Sadie a bit longer and wanting to chop the heads off the little nutcrackers who worked for him. "I'm so sorry. Cleaning the walkways, and ensuring they're safe, is moving to the top of my to-do list."

"It's all part of being on a working ranch, or farm. I'm used to it. That's why I wear sturdy boots." Sadie held her foot out and began to wiggle it to catch Cody's attention. She smiled at him, and Cody's heart thudded in his chest.

He hesitated a moment, then had to clear the fog from his mind. What was going on with him?

Chapter 4

S adie sat outside the Frenchtown Roasting Company, watching the kids and their families walking around in costumes. Halloween had come very quickly, and she had no idea how she was going to get everything done. Not only did she have a lot of work on her own family ranch, but she was still working with Cody on setting up his Christmas tree farm carnival.

They had decided that each weekend they would have something different going on, since they didn't have enough inside space to do all the activities through the entire season.

Lottie Hamilton walked out with a special treat for Sadie. "Here, give this a try. I've got a few treats just for today on the menu." The owner of the popular coffee shop had recently married Cove, a rodeo star whom she had known most of her life. The entire town had been so excited to see the two of them finally marry.

Sadie took the offered dish. "What is it?"

On the plate was a chocolate croissant with orange chocolate drizzled over the top and a few Halloween-shaped sprinkles and a scoop of ice cream on the side. "It's my latest creation, pumpkin croissant à la mode. What do you think?"

The scent coming from the warmed-up pastry wafted into Sadie's nose and she took in a giant sniff. "Mmmm, this smells divine." She noticed that the ice cream was starting to melt even though it wasn't a warm day. There were a few clouds in the sky and the temperature had to be in the upper sixties. It was a perfect day for costumes and trick-or-treating.

Sadie took a small bite, making sure to get the orange drizzle along with a few sprinkles and a small amount of ice cream. The moan that came out of her mouth caught her by surprise. "Oh, that is fantastic. You should have brought this out sooner. How long will you be selling this?"

"You really liked it? There isn't too much orange in the chocolate? It doesn't overpower it, does it?" Lottie bit her lip. This was the first time she had created this particular item. "I just came up with the idea in the middle of the night and then forgot about it. But when I got in today, the idea kept haunting me and it wouldn't stop until I made it."

Both ladies chuckled and Sadie took another bite—this time a much larger one. She nodded and closed her eyes, savoring the flavors of the buttery pastry mixed with the ice cream and the light orange-chocolate flavor. "I love that you used vanilla bean ice cream instead of plain vanilla. There's something about the ground up beans inside the ice cream that makes it creamier. It acts as a bridge between all of the rich flavors and brings them back together on the tongue in such a way to make all of my senses stand up and notice. Seriously, this should be on the menu all year. Maybe you can change up the sprinkles to match the season? And the color of the chocolate can change as well?"

Lottie put a finger to her chin. "Hm, that's not a bad idea. I'll see about getting some pumpkin-only sprinkles. I don't think folks will care to have bats and ghost sprinkles with their pastry in November." She grinned.

Sadie stifled a laugh when she put another bite in her mouth. Talking around the food, she said, "I think most people won't care what kind of sprinkles are on top, just as long as it tastes like this. I think you have another winner on your hands."

"Well, I had to do something to compete with your huckleberry scones. I tried one and they are to die for." Lottie licked her lips. "Do you think you could share your recipe with me?"

A cough escaped along with a few bits of the croissant, and Sadie began coughing harder.

Lottie patted her back. "Do you need some water? Are you alright?"

Sadie shook her head. With a hoarse voice, she replied, "No, I'm fine." She coughed a few more times before taking a sip of her pumpkin latte. "Just about choked when you asked me for my recipe. I don't think I've ever had anyone who bakes as well as you do ask me for a recipe. It just shocked me, that's all."

Cody walked up and grinned at Sadie and Lottie. "Ladies." He tipped his Stetson and looked between the two. "How are you on this fine Halloween day?"

Sadie took a napkin and wiped her mouth.

"I'm doing great, thanks Cody." Lottie looked between the two. "But I must get back inside. Before I go, can I get you anything? A latte? Or perhaps a slice of pie?"

"No, thanks. I'm good." The sheepish grin that crossed Cody's face told Sadie he was up to something. "I just came from the Sip 'n' Go where I had their last huckleberry scone."

Lottie laughed and waved as she walked back inside.

"You should try Lottie's newest creation—it's a Halloween croissant. But I think she's going to change it up for each season. It's really good. Care for a bite of mine?" Sadie offered up the plate for Cody to see.

"Uh, it looks like it must have been great. I think there's only one or two bites left." An amused grin crossed his face before Cody sat down in the chair next to Sadie. "I actually came by to talk about our plans and see how it's all going."

Just then, a cowboy strode past them with a pig on a leash. Both the cowboy and the pig were dressed up for Halloween as pirates. The cowboy, who also happened to be Sadie's little brother Malachi, waved and smiled as he walked past.

"Wait." Cody put a hand up. "Aren't you guys pig farmers?"

Sadie rolled her eyes. It always happened. People would turn their noses up at her, most looking like a pig's snout, and think she was beneath them. "Yes, we are. And I've heard all the jokes."

"No, I wasn't going to joke." Cody waved his hand in front of him. "Isn't that your brother and his little pot-bellied pig you dress up like a pirate every year for Halloween?"

She almost snorted, but stopped herself by coughing to cover the sound. "Yeah, that's Pirate Spot. He's Malachi's pet pig."

Confusion covered Cody's face and he wiped a hand over his mouth, smoothing down the little bit of scruff covering his face. "Um, you're pig farmers who keep pigs for pets?"

"No, Malachi is studying to be a veterinarian. He's the one with pigs for pets." Sadie clucked her tongue and shook her head. "He's always had pigs for pets, in addition to the horses, frogs, chickens." She started to tick off animal breeds on her fingers. "Oh, and he's also had a pet pygmy goat." She shivered.

A small smile edged up one side of Cody's mouth. "Yup, he sounds as though he was always destined to be a vet." Then he scrunched his nose. "But a pig farmer's son having pet pigs? How long did he get to keep his pets before they ended up…you know…on his breakfast plate?"

Sadie slapped Cody's arm. "Bite your tongue. We'd never butcher one of Malachi's pets. We all know the difference between a pet and food. In fact, his first pet pig died of old age just last year."

"Huh, I'd have never guessed a pig farmer to keep pigs as pets, or let their children do it. How'd it happen?"

"Malachi must have been about six years old when we found him rolling around outside in one of the pig pens." Sadie chuckled and thought back to the day. "He was playing with several of the piglets. It was Malachi's job at the time to take the morning slop out to the pens. He must have seen one of the baby pigs and thought it would be fun to play with."

"Gross, playing in a pigsty? Even a small boy wouldn't enjoy that, would he?" He rubbed his arms and realized the hairs on his forearms were standing on end.

"I don't know about that. But one of those pigs, Hamlet, decided to follow Malachi around. After about a week, it was decided that little Hamlet would be Malachi's pet. The pig had attached himself to my brother and followed him like the pied piper. My parents didn't have the heart to take the piglet away, so once he was weaned from his mother, he came inside and became a house pet for Malachi." She shrugged. "The rest, as they say, is history. Now he rescues mini pigs when owners get in over their heads."

"Hence the little pirate pig?" Cody asked.

"Yes." Sadie chuckled. "Pirate Spot was named so because he's pink with black spots all over. One of which covers an eye like a pirate's patch."

"Is that why the pig seems to be doing a dance to the tune of 'A Pirate's Life for Me' right now?" He pointed to the pig in question as it followed Malachi down the sidewalk with a funny step that looked more like a dance than a pig waddle.

Sadie turned her head and giggled. "Yes, and if you listen carefully, you can tell he's singing along."

Cody's brow furrowed and he looked back at the pig. "He's not singing, he's squealing."

She shook her head. "Nope, listen to his tune. He's singing in cadence with the song. Malachi whistles the tune so much, that Pirate Spot knows it on his own now."

They both stood to watch the procession of little kids dressed up for the holiday. Every year the town sponsored a costume parade for the kids, who also went trick or treating at each store after the parade concluded.

There weren't a lot of kids, but the town and the surrounding farmers and ranchers all turned out to support them.

There were little mermaids in homemade iridescent tails, astronauts wearing helmets that were too big for their heads, and of course, the crowd favorite—firemen. Not to mention all the various little monsters and princesses.

A deep chuckle escaped Cody's lips, and Sadie turned to look at him. She couldn't remember the last time she'd heard Cody Makinaw laugh. And his smile sent tendrils of desire up her arms. All the hairs on her body seemed to stand at attention, just waiting for Cody to turn his smile on her. Even her heart began to beat in a way she couldn't remember ever experiencing. This cowboy was handsome, something she hadn't really thought much about before now.

When Cody looked back at her, a wave of dizziness overcame her and she grabbed his arm to steady herself.

Chapter 5

C ody had been laughing at the mini pig. The little guy couldn't have been more than thirty pounds, but he carried himself as though he weighed two hundred and thirty. And that pig knew he had everyone's attention. Excitement flooded his veins for the first time in forever.

He was having fun.

When was the last time he'd done anything except for work or worrying about the tree farm? Sure, he'd enjoyed the huckleberry treats and talking to Sadie the past few weeks, but it wasn't something that gave him joy. Not like this little pig who thought he was Captain Jack Sparrow. He even swaggered like a drunk Captain Jack.

In fact, the entire town was laughing and smiling at the little pirate, who had joined the procession. Who'd have ever thought that a little pig could provide so much entertainment and happiness?

Cody turned to share in the laughs with Sadie, since it was her little brother's pig, after all. But the moment she touched him, a fire licked up his arm and down his body to his toes. He stared into her green eyes, as deep as any emerald he'd ever seen, and all life around him stopped. He only had eyes for the woman in front of him.

With a need to be closer to her, he stepped toward her, closing the distance and putting his hand on her arm. His breath hitched, and he watched her as she shuddered. Then desire pooled in her eyes and it washed over his entire being, only stoking the flames engulfing him.

When he felt a hand slap his back, he was brought back to his surroundings. Cody turned to see Jackson McKinley, Sadie's brother, staring daggers at him. "What's going on here?"

Cody jumped back and gulped, feeling his Adam's apple bob up and down. "We were just, ah, just watching your brother's pig dance down the street."

Jackson grunted. "That's not what it looked like to me."

"Jackson, leave them be," Anita, Jackson's wife, whispered. Then she pulled her husband's hand. "Come on, we're running late."

"Late? For what?" Jackson turned angry eyes on his wife, who only sighed and shook her head.

"Men, I swear. I don't know how your species has survived this long. Come on, leave Sadie and Cody alone." She tugged on Jackson's hand and he started walking.

With two fingers, Jackson pointed from his eyes to Cody's. "I'm watching you, Makinaw." Then he took off following his new bride.

After watching Jackson walk away, Cody turned to Sadie. "Your brother's a bit strange."

Pink tinged Sadie's cheeks, only making Cody realize how beautiful the woman was. He'd never noticed her beauty before. Well, that wasn't exactly true. He'd noticed, but it hadn't hit him until today.

A nervous giggle escaped. "Yeah, he is." She bit her lower lip, drawing his attention. Then she looked away.

He cleared his throat and reminded himself he had business to attend to. Then he made his excuses and fled.

What in the world had just happened? One moment Cody was laughing and enjoying the scene—the kids in the parade, the little pig and his master—then the next he was on fire, figuratively of course. And before he knew it, he felt himself moving closer to Sadie. Was he going to kiss her? Surely he wouldn't have done that, would he?

Craziness, that's all it was. It was a cut-and-dry case of insanity. It ran in his family, didn't it? His grandpops was a bit touched in the head, wasn't he? Cody's parents died young, so he couldn't tell if they were nutjobs. Maybe their early demise and the stress of managing the Christmas tree farm had driven him mad?

Or was it the radiant beauty?

All Cody knew was that he needed her help. She had offered to help him and he couldn't afford to turn her down. But could he afford to spend a lot of time with her? Jackson didn't seem happy that they'd been standing together on the sidewalk in town.

Okay, okay, so maybe Jackson was worried that he'd kiss Sadie in public. That's what he was about to do, wasn't it? Cody ran a hand down his face and blew out a breath. "What am I going to do?"

"About what?" Walking up to Cody was his old friend Mack Stinson, the owner of the town's only auto shop.

Cody stood up straight and looked around. "Huh?"

"You just asked me what you were going to do," Mack said.

"Sorry, I must have been talking to myself." Cody chuckled and started to walk past his friend.

"Hey, wait a second." Mack turned to follow his friend. "Did you want to join us tonight for dinner? It's mac 'n' cheese night. But I've got some bacon to add for those of us who need real protein." He grinned.

"Aren't you taking the kids trick-or-treating?" Cody knew that most families came to town with their kids on Halloween. The stores had candy for those who dressed up and said, "Trick or treat," in an effort to keep kids safe. In some towns, the local churches did a trick-or-trunk event, where car owners parked in the church parking lot and opened their trunks that were full of goodies. But in Frenchtown, things were small. So the local businesses stayed open late and families brought their kids around.

"Sure we are. But once it's all over, we'll head back for dinner. It shouldn't take more than an hour to hit up all the stores and talk to everyone. I figured we'll eat about seven."

"Okay, thanks. I think I'd like that. Plus, I have a few things I wanted to run past you about the upcoming Christmas events out at my farm." Cody hadn't had a chance yet to get all the different booths manned, and he hoped Mack could help out. Maybe even his kids would want to help.

When Mack moved on, Cody saw his farm foreman, Daniel Caruthers. His uncle was the town's veterinarian. "Hey Daniel." He waved over his employee and friend.

Daniel was a few years younger than Cody, but he was tall. He had red hair and blue eyes. Cody appreciated his work ethic; the man worked long and hard on the tree farm. Instead of living on the farm like most foremen do, he lived in town with his uncle Steve.

"Cody, what are you doing here?" Daniel eyed his boss warily.

He put his hands up. "Don't worry, I didn't come to drag you back to the farm. I came into town to talk with Sadie about the marketing for our events."

Daniel grinned. "For a moment I thought you might have actually decided to do something fun for a change."

Little wrinkle lines developed between Cody's eyes. "I know how to have fun." He sounded more like a petulant kid than a grown man disagreeing with a friend.

A deep chuckle escaped Daniel's mouth, attracting the attention of a group of cowboys and one cowgirl, who eyed

Daniel up and down. He winked at her and gave her a sly smile.

One thing was for sure, Daniel wasn't shy when it came to the ladies. The fact that he rarely dated was only because he had such high standards for himself.

The cowgirl raised her chin and walked on without a word or backward glance.

Cody watched the exchange with interest. "She's cute. Do you know her?"

Daniel shook his head. "Nope, never seen her before. But those men she was with were from the Crooked Arrow Ranch."

With wide eyes, Cody turned to watch them as they all walked away. "Really? Do you think she's a wounded vet, too?"

"I doubt it. She didn't look like she was injured. Maybe she's the maid?" Daniel turned back to Cody and grinned.

"What a jingleberry you are." Cody rolled his eyes and shook his head. "Just because she doesn't have any physical signs of injury doesn't mean she's not injured. She could be on the mend, or it could be PTSD. I heard most of the residents of the Crooked Arrow are dealing with trauma from the fighting. Not all injuries are obvious."

"Huh, I guess I never thought about that. I've met a few of the men from the ranch. They seem alright, but don't like loud noises or surprises. I heard they were thinking about bringing in cows to help, kinda like what they do with horses. Just no riding." Daniel scratched his chin and looked back at the woman. She had walked so far down the main street he could barely see her anymore.

"I've heard of the cow cuddling. It's for everyone, not just those suffering from PTSD." Cody had looked into the option, but decided he didn't have the room, or staff, to make it work. At least not this year.

"Cow cuddling?" Daniel snorted. "Are you serious? What, do they actually go and lay down with a cow and wrap their arms around it?"

As serious as ever, Cody turned narrowed eyes on his friend. "Yes, they do. It's now considered a real option to help people with anxiety. And it's rather popular. In fact, I just read an article about one study being done with cows and children who have Down syndrome. They're even talking about it helping kids on the spectrum."

"Really?" Daniel turned wide eyes back on his friend. "Autistic kids are seeing improvement from hugging a cow?"

"It's not just hugging. It's spending time with a cow. Some talk to them, others just sit there petting the cow. Kinda like a pet, but big like a human. I think there's something about the size of the cow. Plus, cows are very loving and sociable. They're like a giant dog, just not as excitable." The idea of cuddling a cow appealed to Cody. Especially lately with all the anxiety he was feeling over the upcoming months, and the costs of it all. He wasn't sure if he would even make it to January without having a breakdown.

The idea of being the last Makinaw to run the family farm really weighed heavily on him. He knew that the lots who bought their trees from him would find other tree farms if he went under, or maybe the new owners of the ranch would be able to keep going. So that part wasn't what bothered him.

What bothered him so much was the idea of losing the family business. A business that had once thrived before he took over. Cody didn't think he'd run the farm into the ground. Just the opposite, he'd actually made a lot of improvements. He'd even started a new line of trees—blue spruce—that should start selling next year.

If he kept the farm, that was.

It wasn't anything he'd done wrong, per se. No, it was that he hadn't thought to diversify. His parents did other things, like crafts. And his dad had even mentioned making the farm into more of a theme park that only ran in November and December

—something he should have done years ago. He only hoped he wasn't too late with implementing some of his parents' ideas.

And then there was the one Sadie had suggested. That one had him on his knees praying for the first time in years, as well as using his weights again.

Chapter 6

After Sadie had said goodbye to Cody, she walked around and looked at the various cowboys of Frenchtown. She hadn't realized how many sexy men they had. Why hadn't she noticed before? Sure, some of them were married or on their way to being married, but a good portion of the single men in town were good looking.

However, since leaving Seattle earlier this year she hadn't been interested in dating. Not after how Wesley had treated her. She was still mad at him for breaking up with her just because she'd lost her job and couldn't find another one. It wasn't like companies were doing much hiring at the moment. There were more and more marketing people out of jobs these days. So the few open positions in her field were tough to get. Men and women who were more qualified than her applied to the same positions she did.

That was one of the reasons she'd moved home earlier this year, to get away from Wesley and all the memories they had shared in Seattle. Plus, living with her parents was free and made it possible for her to start up her own little marketing firm. Currently, she was busier than she could handle. But, it wasn't all from paying clients. She helped her parents on their ranch part-time.

But the biggest draw of her time was Cody.

Being forced to leave town without any job prospects seemed to be a blessing in disguise. Now, she had her own business. She was her own boss and didn't have to listen to stiff-necked people who didn't appreciate her more wholesome ideas. Shoot, she'd even taken one of her clients with her. In the new year she was going to start reaching out to more of her old clients and see if they were still happy with her old firm. Most of them had more wholesome values than the majority of the clients at her old job. So maybe they'd appreciate a marketing expert who aligned more with them than with the worldly Sullivan and Pointers marketing firm.

Sadie had to remind herself why she was looking at the men of Frenchtown. She still needed four more models for her Cowboys of Montana calendar. She almost laughed when she thought back to how Cody had reacted when she told him her idea.

Currently, she had Cody, Malachi, Cove Hamilton, Brandon Beck, and Jake Johnson. Jake was super easy to get on board; he'd jumped at the chance to show off his good looks. The man was so in love with himself, Sadie was surprised he hadn't already found a way to be in a calendar.

She also had asked Tad Jeffries, one of the local ranchers, and Jerod Stevens. He was a former special-ops soldier who ran the Crooked Arrow Ranch. He was probably the most difficult to recruit so far, Cody being a close second.

The foreman over at the Martinez ranch, Javier, was also on board. Now she just needed to find four more men willing to show off their skills for the camera. Not to mention their good looks. All calendars had a fireman, so she'd have to ask Ned, who was married. But he was also the only one who was good looking and young. She almost snorted when she thought about asking the fire chief, Ben. Although, he was a bit of a silver fox. Maybe some of the older set would be tempted to buy the calendar for a look at him in action? Now that she thought more about it, she could have two firemen. One could never have enough firemen, right?

All she needed now were two more volunteers. And she had no idea who to use for December other than Santa. She had gone back and forth on that idea for a few days now. She loved the idea, but if they were going to get a lot of women buying the calendar, would they want an old Santa in December? Chris Lambton was good looking, but old.

Sadie had been looking down at her notepad and didn't notice someone else coming her way who was also looking down at her phone. When they collided, Sadie dropped her notepad and jumped. "Oh, I'm so sorry. I know better than to walk and look down."

"Don't worry about it. I was doing something wrong, too." Chloe laughed and leaned down to pick up her cell phone that she'd had her nose in. She also picked up Sadie's notepad before the woman had a chance.

Chloe read the page and smiled from ear to ear. "Oh, I heard you were planning on making a calendar of our hottest men." She counted the names on the list. "But I don't see twelve. Do you have them all yet?"

"Not yet. But how do you feel about Brandon posing for the calendar? Does it bother you?" Sadie had worried how Chloe might feel. Since they had only recently met, Sadie wasn't sure what the town's medical billing manager would think about her fiancé posing for a hottie calendar.

"It's not like he's going to be shirtless. He told me you asked him to wear chaps over his jeans, and he had to wear something warm since you wanted him to be in a snow-covered field on a horse." Chloe grinned. "I'm actually excited to see my man in a beefcake calendar. It'll be one of those things I pull out every so often and tease him with. Or show off to the kids when they get a bit older, maybe even in high school."

Sadie laughed. "Oh, I'd have been so embarrassed back in high school if my dad had posed for a calendar."

Chloe slapped her palms and pointed at Sadie. "Exactly! I can't wait." She giggled.

"Well, I do still need two more volunteers. I need someone for September. I was thinking about a teacher. You know, back to school and all that." Sadie wrote a couple of notes on her pad, then looked back up at Chloe, who was deep in thought.

"Hmm, what about a doctor? We have that traveling doc who's covering right now until we can find a replacement for one of our doctors who just retired. He's nice looking and sorta young." Chloe pursed her lips. "Well, he's in his forties, but he looks like he could easily pass for thirty. And his thick blond hair always gets women checking him out."

Sadie had to think for a moment. "Oh, you mean the guy with the wavy blond hair? Looks kinda like a Ken doll?"

"Yes, that's the one. He even has the tan to go with his blond locks right now. I think his last assignment was in LA. Doctor Kenneth Eastman is his name, ironically enough."

"Oh, that might be nice. Better than a teacher." Sadie considered. "Unless you count that new one I saw last week. What was his name? Dallas something or other."

Chloe nodded. "You said you needed two. Why not use them both?"

Sadie's nose scrunched up. "I was thinking about having Santa pose for December. Do you think people will want a calendar with an authentic Santa for the last month?"

"Santa in December is perfect." Chloe looked around, then waved Lottie over. "Lottie, we're talking about the calendar."

"Oh, I'm excited for this. Cove isn't as much, but I told him he had to do it." Lottie looked around. "Do you think I could get a few of the extra prints for my own use?"

Sadie and Chloe laughed. "Why? Are you going to make your own pinup calendar of your new husband?"

Lottie grinned and shook her head. "No, nothing like that. I was just thinking it would be fun to have some framed and put up. Cove said you were going to get pics of him on a bull. Is that right?"

Sadie nodded. "Yup, it only makes sense since he was a champion bull rider before he retired earlier this year."

"Exactly. So is that a yes?" Lottie put her hands together in a begging gesture.

Sadie wished she had a man to love as much as Lottie seemed to love Cove. "Yeah, I think I'll give all the extra copies to each pinup guy. The only ones I won't give out are the images we use for the calendar."

"That's fair." The evil glint that entered Lottie's eyes caused Sadie to pause and wonder if this request was spurred on by love or something else entirely.

"What's going through your head? I recognize that look." Sadie arched a brow.

Chloe crossed her arms over her chest. "I think she's got something up her sleeves."

"Nothing I can talk about, just a Christmas present idea." Lottie waved to her friends and walked off before either could ask any more.

"What do you think she's up to?" Chloe asked.

Sadie shook her head. "I don't know. And quite frankly, I'm not sure I want to know."

Chapter 7

I t was the first weekend in November, and they had two feet of snow on the ground. Cody couldn't believe his luck. It was the weekend they were going to open the tree farm. He didn't expect people would buy trees yet, but it was a chance for them to pre-order and reserve the tree they wanted. As well as a chance to ride the sleigh, now that they had the snow. And a few of the ladies from church had brought in booths to sell crafts, in addition to the couple Cody and Daniel had already built.

The craft fair was a last-minute addition to the lineup. Sadie had said she could post it on social media and have the local city offices post it to their social media pages as well as their websites. Most cities now had a monthly calendar of events that they kept up to date. Some even emailed the citizens with a link to their calendars.

All of this technology still confused Cody, but he knew from his own experience, that it worked.

Sadie had spoken to all the city managers within a two-hour drive of the tree farm. They were not only going to add all events to their calendars, but most were even going to do a feature article on some of the different events. She had most weekends covered by either a city posting, an ad in a local newspaper, or various social media influencers from the area. She even got the local news to agree to come out next weekend and do a special report on the tree farm and all the events coming up, as well as talk about the calendar.

The local weather girl was all excited to see the calendar when it was completed. She had even asked if she could come to the photoshoot, which was scheduled for last week and finishing up this week. They should have the first batch of printed calendars by next weekend, and if they needed another one, the printer said they could get it done quickly.

Daniel pulled up in the sleigh to take the first group out for a ride around the edges of the tree farm. "Hey, Cody. It's looking good for our first day, isn't it?"

A grim-faced cowboy with a black Stetson looked up to the ranch foreman. "Yes, I do think we're going to have a larger turnout than expected."

"Then why so grim?" Daniel stood up and prepared to dismount the front of the sleigh. "You should be happy with a good turnout."

"I know, but now I'm wondering what's going to go wrong. I don't see how this day can go smoothly. Especially with all of these people." Cody took off his hat and ran a hand through his already messy hair. "I keep thinking I forgot something, but I just don't know what it is."

Daniel chuckled. "Don't worry, I think Sadie has it all in hand. That woman is amazing. I can't believe how she's been able to get so much organized so quickly."

"I think that's part of my problem."

"How so?" Daniel put the brake on the sleigh and tied off the horses' reins.

"So much is happening so quickly. And she's just one person. I doubt I've hired enough people to man this event." Cody shrugged. "I guess I'm just waiting for the other boot to drop."

"Oh come on, think more positively. It all could go quite well. And maybe you'll even make some money on this venture." Daniel knew how tough the farm's financial situation was. He knew that come the new year, he might be out of a job. Although, he'd probably be the last one let go if Cody needed to start laying off employees.

"We shall see," was all Cody could say.

The first family to buy tickets for a sleigh ride came up, and Daniel helped them into the sleigh. "See ya later, boss."

Cody grunted.

Before Daniel got up in the sleigh, he looked back at Cody. "Dude, cheer up. It's Christmas." Then Daniel jumped up into the sleigh and took off at a slow pace, the bells on the sleigh ringing in the sounds of Christmas.

Music began playing through the speakers Cody and his team had recently set up for the season. Trumpet sounds from "O Come All Ye Faithful" by Nat King Cole came out, and Cody began to relax.

Chapter 8

Sadie walked out of the barn with a big smile on her face. She loved Nat King Cole's Christmas music. Especially the song playing at that moment. She couldn't help it—the words came out of her mouth. As she walked around the corner, she was just singing, "born the king of angels" when she bumped into a brick wall.

"Whoa, I didn't realize we were doing Christmas karaoke now." For the second time that week, Cody chuckled and grinned at Sadie. This wasn't the first time he'd caught her singing to the sounds of Christmas music. Unfortunately for her, she didn't exactly get the key right.

While Sadie knew she'd never get on any of those reality singing shows, she still loved to sing. And she knew she couldn't carry a tune to save her life, so she normally kept her singing to times when she was alone, like when she drove out to the Christmas tree farm. But for some reason, she felt the joy of the season bubbling up from her core and she had to sing along with Nat.

Sadly, it just happened to be when she ran into Cody. The tall, handsome cowboy who seemed to send her heart singing every time she saw him was as fit as a bodybuilder. Sadie felt heat burning its way up her neck and into her face. All she could do was hope she looked red from the cold and not from embarrassment.

"Ah, sorry about that. I didn't think anyone was over in this area." Sadie looked around and realized they were alone out back behind the barn.

"No worries. I like singing to Christmas music, too." Only Cody kept his singing confined to the shower, where there wasn't a chance anyone could hear him.

She clicked her tongue. "Yeah, well, ah, I better get going." She looked around, trying to find something she had to do. "Um, I have a…thing to go do." And she practically ran past him.

A deep, warm chuckle escaped him, and Cody shook his head. He headed back to the locked storeroom where he kept the insulated coffee mugs they sold at the tree farm during Christmas. It featured the old farmhouse-style red truck that had been so popular the past few years, and the words *Big Sky Christmas* were printed on it. Tourists especially loved to buy these mugs. The local Sip 'n' Go also stocked them and sold them in droves with their coffee. He didn't have the best margins on this product, but it was something he had already paid for, so all money he made this year from sales was profit. Something he liked to see on his spreadsheets.

Sadie had asked if there was a way to increase the price he offered to the Sip 'n' Go so his profit margins were a bit better, but he had told her the price was already set. However, since they also sold them at the tree farm, Sadie used this as another item to attract attention. If they sold the insulated mug at the same price as the Sip 'n' Go, then they would make much more profit. So she talked Cody into offering free coffee all season to anyone who bought the mug from the tree farm. They just had to keep the receipt and show it each time they came out. And maybe, just maybe, this would get some of the local families to come out more than once.

The moment Cody was out of her sight, Sadie breathed a sigh of relief. She didn't know what was going on, but that cute cowboy had gotten under her skin. And she didn't like it. Not one bit.

Her ears perked up when she heard Burl Ives singing, "You better watch out, and you better not cry…".

"Santa Claus is Coming to Town" was one of Sadie's favorite songs. And she always watched the Claymation movie, too. Christmas was her favorite time of the year; she loved how everyone always seemed just a bit nicer. People also attended church more often. But the best part was the true meaning of Christmas. She loved that it was the time of year that she was able to openly celebrate the birth of her Lord and Savior.

Of course, she loved Santa and Frosty, and all of the other worldly displays of Christmas. It just made it more fun. But she never forgot it was Jesus's birthday. This year, she still hadn't figured out what she was going to get Jesus for his birthday, but it would come to her.

Last year, she spent three different Saturdays at the Seattle homeless shelter down by Pike's Place Market. She served meals and spent time talking to the moms and their kids. That time with those poor families was what she still remembered in her heart. While Frenchtown didn't have any homeless people, they did have a ranch that specialized in helping veterans. Maybe she could find a way to help them?

It was crazy how God worked.

Sadie chuckled to herself as she watched Megan Anderson and several of the guests of the Crooked Arrow Ranch come up to the barn where they were selling hot drinks and the insulated coffee mugs. Megan was a counselor for the veterans who came to recover from various injuries and issues.

The snow crunched beneath Sadie's boots as "Winter Wonderland" played over the speakers, and she caught herself before she started singing along in front of anyone. She wasn't about to embarrass herself again.

"Megan, it's so good to see you out here. Are you having fun?" Sadie looked from the brown-haired woman with brown eyes to the three men in her company. They were a bit haggard. None of them had shaved in a while, and their beards made them look like mountain men.

"Sadie, hey there. Everything looks so wonderful. Like a picture-perfect winter wonderland. How'd you do this?" Megan grinned and motioned to the scene around them.

The barn was red, and snow covered the roof with at least an inch of fresh powder. Around them, the Christmas trees as well as the local pine trees were dusted with the fresh snow. The pine scent mixed with the clean snow and fresh mountain air helped to instill in Sadie a feeling of health and, oddly enough, openness. It really was like something out of a Norman Rockwell painting. Sadie felt as though she belonged here. It was home.

When she lived in Seattle, everything was so close. She felt as though everyone lived right on top of each other. In some cases, they did. And she had thought her 900-square-foot apartment was spacious at the time. Now she knew it was tiny in comparison to a sprawling Christmas tree farm. Or in her family's case, a pig farm.

"Me?" Sadie touched her chest and opened her eyes wide. "It wasn't me. This was all Cody and Daniel, as well as a bevy of volunteers and a handful of employees. I think the entire town was excited to see Christmas come early this year."

One of the scroungy, bearded men next to Megan coughed.

"Oh, where are my manners? Sorry. Sadie, let me introduce you to my ranch-mates." Megan pointed to the tallest of the bunch. "This is Sam Marley." Then she motioned to a man on crutches. "This here hellion is Skeeter Murphy." And the final man she introduced stood off to the side and a bit behind Sam. "This is Mike Blakenship."

Sadie nodded and smiled at them. "It's very nice to meet y'all. How do you like the ranch life?"

Mike shrugged his shoulders.

Megan noticed and grinned. "Don't believe Mike's nonchalant attitude. He loves milking the cows, and you should try his butter. It's so smooth and creamy. You'd think he grew up on a dairy farm."

Pink tinged Mike's cheeks, and he seemed to tuck more into himself. Sadie noticed he had longer, curly, black hair with the ends that curled over the top of his shirt collar. She also noted the soft, brown eyes of the man almost hiding himself from her.

"Well, I'd love to try the butter. Freshly made butter is something I've grown up with, but missed out on when I lived in Seattle." Sadie put her hand out to shake, but Mike ignored her attempt at friendliness. She hoped she wasn't offending him. All she wanted was to make him feel welcome.

"Oh, come on, Mike. The little lady just wants to be your friend." Skeeter pushed Mike's shoulder, then he walked up to Sadie and offered his work-worn hand. It was obvious this man had seen a lot of hard labor. His hands were already covered in calloused. "It's very nice to make your acquaintance. And please, ignore Megan. I'm the nicest one of the bunch." His grin was almost covered up by the scraggly mountain-man-esque beard. He pointed to Sam. "Now, he's the one you have to watch out for." He put his hand up to his mouth and said sotto voce, "He's known to be a real Grinch."

Sadie couldn't help the chuckle that escaped. She thought she was going to like Skeeter. "Oh, so you're just the resident friendly mountain man?" She arched a brow.

Sam grumbled and shoved Skeeter away, who wobbled a bit on his crutches and glared at Sam. "Ignore him, ma'am. He's the one you need to be careful of, he thinks he's a real Don Juan.

You'll never need worry about me. I've sworn off women for all time."

Sam had a prosthetic left arm that he tried to cover up by wearing long sleeves and gloves. But Sadie had seen the space between his glove and shirt sleeve. While his wrist was a shade of tan skin, the prosthesis wasn't of the highest quality and therefore it was obvious that Sam had lost his arm. While Sadie wanted to get a better look, she had heard enough stories to know that one should never stare at an amputee. It was the height of rudeness.

Sadie wondered what Sam's story was. However, she knew enough about the residents of the ranch to not ask. At least, not until she knew them better. If she had to guess, Skeeter was a player. Definitely one to stay away from, but he'd probably be a hoot. Mike would probably be someone who rarely spoke. And Sam, well that poor man had probably lost his girl when he lost his arm. While she'd never dump a man for losing a limb, especially one who lost it serving his country, she knew plenty of women who wouldn't want anything to do with a man who wasn't what society deemed 100% healthy. Which was too bad; Sam seemed like he used to be a soulful gentleman.

"All time?" Sadie closed her mouth, not wanting to say what she really thought. Sam only needed the right woman to come along and then he'd probably never say he'd sworn them off for *all* time, just a *short* time.

He narrowed his eyes. "Now don't go getting any ideas about me 'n' you. Not gonna happen."

Skeeter couldn't be outdone. "Of course not. Because I'm the one who's gonna steal this pretty little lady's heart. Not some ornery ol' coot."

When Skeeter grinned at Sadie, she shook her head. "I think Sam may have been right about you, Skeeter."

"What about Skeeter?" Cody walked up and tipped his hat to Megan. "Miss Megan, good to see you again."

"Cody, always a pleasure." Megan grinned at him but scowled at Daniel, who had been standing next to Cody.

Sadie wondered about those two. She hadn't heard anything, but from the look Megan gave the Christmas tree farm foreman, there had to be a story behind it.

"Why Megan, I'm just as happy to see you as you are to see me." Daniel winked at her, and Sadie could see Megan's skin crawl as she shivered. Or was it goosebumps that were going all up and down Megan's body? Sadie would have to get to the bottom of that one.

Mr. and Mrs. Claus walked up before Sadie had a chance to say anything else.

Christopher Lambton, affectionately known at Mr. Claus by the town, was dressed in his Santa suit. With black boots, red triangle hat with white faux fur, and a black belt with a giant golden buckle that looked as though it had been shined to perfection, any Santa would have been impressed.

"Sadie and Megan, it's wonderful to see you both again." Jessica Lambton, AKA Mrs. Claus, greeted the two women before looking to the men in the group. "I say, we've got a wonderful group of cowboys here today, don't we Santa?"

"Ho, ho, ho. I'd say so." Santa laughed and his belly full of jelly danced under his hands. "Are y'all here to help run the events this weekend?"

Sadie had asked Jerod Stevens—the owner of the Crooked Arrow Ranch, which was where wounded vets went after being discharged for severe medical issues—if he had anyone who wanted to help out. Jerod told her he'd send a few over to help. But she didn't think Sam and Mike would be interested. As for Skeeter, he'd probably spend more time flirting with the young women than working.

But they were volunteering this weekend, not paid employees. She'd have to remember that.

Chapter 9

W hen Cody walked up to the group gathered before him, he wasn't sure what to expect. He'd overheard that scoundrel, Skeeter, trying to flirt with Sadie and felt a bit miffed. Then he had to remind himself that she wasn't his girl. She was only helping him out. If she wanted to flirt with a man who needed help caring for his scruff that was trying to be a beard, then she could. He had no claims on her. None whatsoever.

But when he noticed the tension between Daniel and Megan was so thick that not even a knife would cut it, he had to do a double take.

Thank goodness for Santa and Mrs. Claus. They could always be counted on to ease any tension and turn a bad situation to good.

"Santa, it's so good of you to come out, and dressed to the nines, too." He reached out to take Mrs. Claus's hand and kissed the back of it. "Mrs. Claus, you always add such elegance to our events. Have you been out on the sleigh yet? I'd love to take you myself and maybe even get a few pictures of you and Santa out in the snow between the trees?"

Jessica clapped her hands and smiled at Cody. "That is a wonderful idea. You should use the pictures for your marketing efforts." She eyed Sadie. "And maybe you could come too, to take the pictures? Or at least let us know what would work best for your campaigns?"

Cody had known the Lambtons his entire life. As a little boy he always went and sat on Santa's lap and told him what he wanted for Christmas. And lo and behold, he would find it wrapped in special paper under his tree Christmas morning. It wasn't until he went away to college that he learned most kids stopped believing in Santa around the age of ten. Some were older, but most stopped believing too early and therefore lost the fun of the season. Sure, he knew and understood that it was Jesus's birthday, but lately he hadn't really thought much about Jesus, or even attended church regularly. It was all he could do to get up each morning and get his work done.

But this year, everything felt different. He could feel the magic in the air. God was another story altogether, but he was going to make an effort to attend church as much as possible. He'd probably only get to a few Sunday night services since they opened at eleven Sunday mornings. He'd need to be there to help open the grounds and the lot. He wasn't alone in the need to work Sunday mornings; most cowboys or ranch owners either came in late on Sunday mornings or only attended the evening services.

He tuned back in to the conversation between Sadie and Jessica and realized that Mrs. Claus had invited Sadie to join them on a sleigh ride. Sure, it was for picture-taking, but he'd get to enjoy the holiday ride with a beautiful woman. How'd he ever get so lucky?

"When do you want to do this? Now?" Cody asked. "Or would you prefer to come out one day this week when there's no one else around?"

Santa looked around and noticed all the people coming in and the line for the sleigh rides. "I think we could schedule a time during the week that's convenient for everyone. Looks like you're already getting busy, my boy." He pointed to the crowds forming behind Cody. "And I'd hate to take away from any opportunity to sell sleigh rides."

As he turned around to see what Santa was pointing to, Cody realized he had blocked out the sounds emanating from the many families behind him. "Wow, I didn't even realize that many people had arrived already." A half smile touched his cheek and he quickly extinguished it. "I'm available any day after the animals have been fed."

"And I can come out any time," Sadie offered. "I don't really have a set schedule these days."

"Well, we have to finish up the calendar shoots. So, how about Wednesday afternoon? I hear we're due for another snowstorm Tuesday night, so the snow will be fresh and pristine come Wednesday." Normally Cody wasn't too keen on multiple snowstorms before Thanksgiving, but with his sleigh-ride business already off to a great start, maybe it would be a good thing to have a lot of snow this year.

When Sunday evening came around and they closed up the barn for the day, Cody considered his plan to attend Sunday evening services. He had promised himself, and God, that he'd attend. He knew his grandpops enjoyed attending services, but he was so tired after the harried weekend.

Word had gotten out about their sleigh rides and the fact that if you came out and picked out a tree early, you could get a discount. So of course a lot of people had come out this weekend. Which meant that he'd probably have a lot coming next weekend as well.

Mrs. Denning walked up to him and smiled. "Cody, thank you for suggesting that the quilting circle set up shop here. We've sold quite a few quilts and samplers in just the few hours we've been here. I'd be surprised if we have anything left by the end of this month."

"I had no idea this would go so well. Do you have some stock set aside for the town's craft fair in December? I'd hate to sell everyone's crafts here before the really big event." He really didn't *hate* the idea. He kinda liked it. If the town's ladies sold all of their crafts here this year, then they'd work harder next year and have an even larger supply to sell. Which would mean more crafters would set up shop here, and then more money for him.

The deep laugh emanating from Mrs. Denning surprised Cody. Didn't women normally put forth a sweet laugh? "Oh, Cody. I'd much rather sell out now and then be able to enjoy the craft fair in town next month. There are a lot of vendors who come from all over to sell, so no worries if we don't have any quilts to sell there." Then she stepped closer and lowered her voice. "Besides, we can sell our quilts here for more money than at the fair. No competition." She waggled her brows and wiggled her fingers as she walked away.

"Devious ladies." Cody shook his head and locked the barn door. Then he headed inside the house to warm up and see what was for dinner. "Grandpops, you here?" Cody yelled when he walked into the mudroom and removed his wet, snowy boots.

"In the kitchen, son," Joseph called out.

The scent of beef stew wafted in along with the pungent smell of fresh-baked sourdough bread. "Wow, I didn't know you could make bread. What's this?" Cody picked up a perfectly browned roll and sniffed. "Mmmm." Then he bit into the warm bread.

Grandpops chuckled. "My boy, don't forget the butter." He handed the tub of freshly churned butter to Cody.

"Where'd you get all of this?" Cody asked.

"One of the church widows brought out the crockpot with stew and the freshly made rolls. All I had to do was pop them in the oven right before dinner." The old man grinned, and Cody noticed he had his good teeth in.

"Did you wear your white dentures for a particular lady?" Cody grinned. He couldn't remember when his grandpops had last cleaned up for a lady.

"Pft." Joseph waved a hand before his face. "I'm all gussied up for church. You said you'd start taking me on Sunday nights. In my day, even the cowboys dressed up in their nicest clothes to attend church."

Cody's face fell. "Oh, yeah. About that…"

"You don't have to dress up. I know today it's common for farmers and ranchers to come as they are Sunday nights. Since you've been working all day, it makes sense." Grandpops poured a bowl of beef stew and set it on the table in front of Cody.

Now Cody felt as though he had to attend church. It wasn't that he didn't believe in God, because he did. He'd grown up attending Sunday services with his folks. But ever since he took over running the tree farm, he just didn't have the energy to attend. It was his one day to rest. And after the success of this weekend, he needed the rest. But, he had promised he'd attend. So he grudgingly finished his dinner and cleaned up enough to attend services.

The main reason he'd stopped attending was because he didn't know how he could praise or worship a God who would take his parents from him so soon. Ever since they died, he'd had nothing but problems.

Problems with finishing school, which he was unable to do—thanks, God.

Problems with the tree farm, which he was most likely going to lose—thanks, God.

Problems with his grandfather's health, who'd be lucky to make it another year—again: thanks, God.

Why couldn't an almighty God make life easier for the likes of Cody Makinaw? His entire family believed in God and even had some relatives who had been pastors. They were all long gone, but still. His family had been servants to God, and this was how the Almighty repaid them?

There were days where he just wanted to run out to the trees and scream at the top of his voice, "Why me? God, why do good people suffer when bad people get all the blessings?"

There was a little niggle in the back of his mind that told him the truth, but he wasn't ready to hear it. So he had skipped out on church because the tree farm needed him more.

Now, however, his grandpops needed him. Cody wasn't about to let the man down. All his life his grandfather had been there for him. Now it was his turn to be there for his grandpops.

As he and his grandpops entered the building, the song "Come Just As You Are" was playing and the parishioners were singing along with it. It was very apropos, since most of the cowboys did, in fact, come as they were. Dirty boots, jeans, and button-up shirts were the dress code for cowboy churches. Only those in his grandfather's generation seemed to still dress up for services. The elderly men still wore their suits with bolo ties while the grandmotherly sort wore dresses with bonnets or hats. Cody liked the hats the women wore; it reminded him of attending services as a kid and paying more attention to the décor in the women's hats than the message.

However, tonight was different. While he did appreciate the ladies' hats, he also listened to the sermon. There must have been a reason that hymn was chosen at the beginning of the service. The pastor was speaking on coming to God just as you are, no need to make any changes to who you were. Jesus even dined with the sinners and publicans of his day.

The pastor read aloud:

"'And Jesus entered and passed through Jericho. And, behold, there was a man named Zacchaeus, which was the chief among the publicans, and he was rich. And he sought to see Jesus who he was: and could not for the press, because he was of little stature. And he ran before, and climbed up into a sycamore tree to see him: for he was to pass that way. And when Jesus came to the place, he looked up, and saw him, and said unto him, Zacchaeus, make haste and come down, for today I must abide at thy house.'"

Luke 19:1-5 told the story of a tax collector named Zacchaeus. Back in these days, the tax collectors collected more than necessary from the people and kept a portion for themselves. They were nothing more than glorified, state-sanctioned thieves.

Zacchaeus knew he wasn't worthy of Jesus's attention, so he climbed a tree in order to get a look at the King of the Jews as he passed by. When, lo and behold, Jesus looked directly up at the thief and invited himself to dinner at the tax collector's house that day.

Jesus knew that the people of the city would think him odd. Some ridiculed him, but Jesus still went to the man's house for dinner. Jesus never asked the man to change his ways. Instead, He shared the gospel message with the man. When Zacchaeus heard the good news of how Jesus had come to save those who were lost, he believed in Jesus and made such changes to the way he did business that it was obvious he had truly accepted who Jesus was, and the saving grace that came along with the knowledge.

The interesting part of the sermon was that Jesus didn't ask Zacchaeus to make any changes. Jesus took him just as he was. The changes came naturally as the man believed in the Lord and chose to serve him, instead of the world and what it thought was important.

Out of the corner of his eye, Cody noticed Sadie as she got up to leave after the sermon was over. He too got up with his grandpops and left the church. Cody knew Sadie was a churchgoer, but he had forgotten that she attended the same church as his family. He had to smirk to himself when he realized that she, too, was wearing her jeans, boots, and a simple yellow-and-white gingham shirt. She had changed her clothes after working all day at the tree farm, but she wasn't wearing a dress. He liked her in jeans.

"So, what did you think of the sermon?" Grandpops asked once they were on their way home.

Cody took a few moments to order his thoughts. "I thought it was interesting timing."

"Oh, how so?" Joseph looked at his grandson out of the corner of his eye and waited for the boy to speak.

"We had just been discussing coming to church dressed how we wanted to. The topic was, 'come as you are.' I'm sure the pastor meant more than just clothes. Since the scripture he used was about an unsaved publican, or tax collector, I'm guessing that the pastor wanted people to realize that they don't have to be perfect, or even good, to come to Jesus."

"That's right, my boy." Grandpops nodded and grinned. "All we have to do is trust in Jesus and he'll take care of the rest. Any changes we need in our lives will happen. The Holy Spirit will guide and direct us."

While Cody knew and understood this, it still didn't answer his question of why God would let such awful things happen to good people. His parents had come to the Lord just as they were when they were kids. Cody didn't know anyone as good as his parents. They had donated to various charities, even went on a few mission trips during the summers. But still, God let them die in a stupid car accident.

And now the tree farm was on the verge of being lost to a family who had served the Lord for generations. Cody didn't think he'd ever understand how a loving God could do this to him and his family.

Chapter 10

The scent of freshly brewed coffee tempted Sadie to enter the Frenchtown Roasting Company, even though she was on a mission. She'd stayed up way too late the night before going through all the images the photographer had taken of their sexy cowboys from Frenchtown. Of course, the images showed the men fully clothed and in the middle of doing various activities that matched their professions. They had firemen, real cowboys, a rodeo star, a doctor, and even Santa Claus.

The only problem she'd had was with Jake Johnson. He was the reason she had been up so late last night. If he would have just listened to direction and done what was asked of him, they would have finished the photoshoot by eight o'clock, just as she'd planned. But no, Jake had to be difficult.

Sadie sighed and headed into the coffee shop. A specialty coffee and a pastry would do her a world of good.

Lottie looked up from the register when she heard the jingle bell above the door. "Sadie, what brings you in this morning?"

She slowly made it to the counter and leaned on her elbows, putting her head in her hands. Through muffled fingers she asked for a latte. "Oh, and one of those new croissants you're making. What are you calling them now that Halloween's over?"

"I actually haven't figured out a name. Quinn wants me to call it the 'Flakes of Fall.'" Lottie shook her head and pursed her lips. Quinn was her little nine-year-old girl whose father had died riding bulls when she was just a baby.

Sadie stood up and smiled. "Of course she does. Little Quinnie always has great ideas." She pursed her lips. "But this time I'd say she needs to go back to the drawing board."

"What about pumpkin croissant?" A deep male voice startled Sadie, and she jumped.

Sadie put a hand to her heart. "Cove. I guess that's one way to wake me up."

"Sorry, Sadie. Rough night?"

She nodded. "You could say that."

"Who came in for their photoshoot last night? Was it one of those rapscallions? If so, I'll go set them straight for ya." Cove grinned and flexed his muscles.

"Whoa now, if you're not careful you'll have all the women of Frenchtown fawning all over your manly arms." Sadie looked to Lottie, who was recently married to Cove, and winked at her friend. Not that Cove wasn't handsome, because he most certainly was. But for some reason, Sadie had never been interested in the former bull rider. He was too outgoing for her taste. No, she preferred her men a bit on the quieter side, not prone to flirting with everyone like Cove always did.

Lottie laughed. "Cove doesn't understand that he's no longer pinup material. He forgets that he retired from the limelight earlier this year."

"Hey now, I'm not completely out of the picture." He grinned at both women. "See what I did there? I'm in the calendar. The calendar picture."

When both women looked at him with stony faces, he threw his hands up and sighed. "I see how it is. Guess I'll have to go and see Brandon in order to get anyone to laugh at my jokes. Oh, was it Brandon who gave you a hard time last night?"

Sadie shook her head. "No, Brandon was just fine. It was the cowboy after him that was difficult."

Cove thought for a moment, then chuckled. "Oh, I should have known. Jake Johnson. What did he do, try to flirt with you all night instead of posing for the camera?"

"No." Sadie sighed. "If only that was the issue. I can deal with a flirtatious man. He kept taking his shirt off, insisting that the pictures of him would be so much better shirtless. And if we put him on the cover, we'd sell out in a heartbeat."

Lottie busted up laughing, and Cove wasn't too far behind her.

"What's so funny?" The voice behind Sadie surprised her, and she stood taller before turning around.

"Cody. I didn't hear you come in." Sadie felt the heat creeping up her neck and knew that everyone could see her embarrassment. Which only made it worse.

"Y'all were laughing too hard to hear the bell. What's so funny? A new joke going around?" Cody looked from Sadie to Cove and Lottie before looking back to Sadie.

"No. Well, sorta." Sadie shrugged. "I was just telling these two about the final photoshoot from last night. Which reminds me, I really need the biggest latte you have along with the pumpkin croissant, or whatever you're going to call it."

Cove looked at the confused expression on Cody's face. "You weren't there for the final shoot?" Cody had been there for most of Cove's shoot. They'd walked out together, but Cody went inside his house instead of back to the barn to watch Jake.

"No, it was getting late and I needed to get a few things done before heading off to bed. What happened?" Cody turned his full attention to Sadie and his brows furrowed.

Sadie waved a hand. "Nothing big. It was just Jake being Jake. He took too long to get into the proper costume. No big deal."

Cove chuckled. "You mean he took too long to get into costume. Period. End of sentence." He turned to look at his friend. "Jake kept insisting on being shirtless."

Stormy gray eyes turned to Sadie, and she noticed he was breathing hard and his teeth were clenched when he spoke. "Was he being inappropriate with you?"

Sadie wasn't sure what he was getting at. Did Cody mean to ask if Jake was trying to get her to roll in the hay with him? She doubted Jake would have tried that. He was more the type to want silk sheets, not a hard floor with old hay that would poke into his pristine skin. "No." She held a hand up. "Nothing like that. He just thought we'd sell more pictures if he was shirtless."

"And on the cover," Lottie added as she handed an extra-large cup of coffee to Sadie.

Sadie took a sip and sighed. "Thank you, Lottie. You are the best." She took another sip. "I thought you were adamant about not serving the Christmas drinks until Thanksgiving?" Her friend had made her an extra-large gingerbread latte, just the way she loved it.

"Ah, think nothing of it." Lottie waved a hand in front of her. "And besides, since we're kinda starting Christmas early, I thought I'd bring out a few of the more popular Christmas drinks. Chloe's been bugging me about the peppermint mochas, too."

Cove put a hand on the counter. "Does this mean you're gonna bring in my favorite treat early as well?"

"Nope, no Christmas treats yet. I still have quite a few pumpkin-themed treats to sell first."

"Oh, yes. You bought that giant case of pumpkin puree. I guess it would be smart to go ahead and sell out of the pumpkin treats before bringing in the ones that everyone will be running to first." Cove was now Lottie's business partner in addition to being her husband. They ran the coffee shop together. He still had a ways to go before he made great lattes, but Sadie knew he'd get it eventually.

Then an idea struck Sadie and Cody at the same time.

"The tree farm?" Sadie looked at Cody, who nodded.

"Why don't you make up a bunch of your pumpkin treats and bring out your cart for the weekends?" Sadie asked Lottie. "At least until Thanksgiving. That way you can sell a bunch of your pumpkin creations, and our guests will have something to keep them there longer." Sadie had considered getting a food truck or coffee truck to come out. But with everything else going on, she hadn't had the time yet to book anyone.

Cove and Lottie looked at each other. Some sort of silent communication passed between husband and wife. Then Lottie turned back to Sadie. "I've got a college student who could use more hours on the weekend."

"And Dana said she wanted more hours during the week," Cove said. "Maybe she can make up the dough for the treats and freeze them all week. On Friday, she could take them out and bake them up for Tessa to bring out on Saturday and Sunday."

Tessa was in her first year of college, thanks partly to the town. They had begun doing monthly fundraisers last Christmas to help the local kids pay for college. And Lottie gave the girl as many hours as she needed on weekends when she was home visiting.

"That would be great." Lottie looked at Cove. "Do you have a covered booth you're not using? I'd rather keep my one and only cart here since it's not really designed for using outside at a ranch. If this goes well, next year we can build our own little shack and then whenever you have any events at the farm, we can open our shack and sell coffee and pastries. We can even bring out premade sandwiches."

"I love this idea. I don't know why we didn't think of it sooner." Sadie grinned at her friends.

"Probably because you're running around like a chicken with its head cut off already." Megan walked up and stood next to Sadie, Cove, and Cody. "Good morning, y'all. Is this the place to congregate for the latest town gossip?"

A small chuckle escaped Sadie's lips. "Not really. We're just discussing ideas for improving the tree farm's offerings this year, and for the future. What did you think of it all this past weekend?"

"I think it needed a specialty coffee booth." Megan put a finger to her chin. "And some basic food options. It wasn't like it was a place to spend the entire day." She turned to Cody. "No offense, but there's just not enough to do out there all day long."

Sadie agreed. "I have more ideas for next year. Including some fall events." She turned to Cody. "Do you have space to grow pumpkins? And maybe even some corn so you can make a corn maze?"

After a short pause, Cody blinked and a small smile began to form on his lips. "I think this might be exactly what I needed. I was hoping to have more sources of income, and a fall festival with a pumpkin patch, corn maze, and some rides would be great. I could set aside a small area off to the side of barn for this. It might take a couple of seasons to get enough pumpkins for a large event, but I could surely do enough for next fall and then have some room for growth."

"I've always loved a good fall festival," Megan said. "I tried to suggest it for the Crooked Arrow Ranch, but Jerod wasn't interested. And he's right, it wouldn't be good for newly arrived residents dealing with PTSD to have to deal with the noises and the people." She grimaced.

"Well, I've really gotta leave and head over to the printer's office," Sadie said. "He has the calendar proof and I have to approve it before he can start the print run. I wanted to get a few hundred calendars ready for this weekend, to sell at the tree farm." Sadie had promised the local weather girl that they'd have the first of the calendars to sell that weekend. And the meteorologist had agreed to do her weather report from the tree farm, and to show off the calendar and let her viewers know where to get their own copy.

"Here, don't forget the pumpkin croissant." Lottie handed her a bag with the fall creation.

Sadie grinned. "I guess this means you've decided on a simple name?"

"For now. We shall see what happens."

"You could always hold a naming contest. Then the winner's name will become part of the croissant's name. You know, like 'Cody's Pumpkin Chip Croissant.' Or something to that effect." Sadie said her goodbyes while Lottie mulled over the name.

"You know, I kinda like it. How about we just go with Sadie's Pumpkin Chip Croissant and call it a day?" Lottie turned to write the new name up on the chalkboard where all the items were listed.

The jingle bell over the door made its Christmas sound as Sadie exited the coffee shop. She wasn't thrilled about her name being in front, but she did think pumpkin chip croissant was a good name. Especially since there was a pumpkin flavor along with some tiny chocolate chips.

Now if only the calendar turned out to be a truly wonderful idea, then she'd call today a success.

Chapter 11

Cody said his goodbyes without getting anything to eat or drink. He had wanted to try that croissant, but he wanted to see the calendar more than anything else. He was still feeling self-conscious about his photoshoot and was anxious to see how his pictures turned out. Sadie and the photographer had both told him he did great. But he wasn't used to being the center of attention.

Would the calendar be an embarrassment to him and the tree farm? Would his parents have approved? Those questions, along with a few more, had been going through his head lately and he needed answers. He knew that no one was shirtless and it wasn't truly a beefcake calendar. At least, it didn't seem like it would sit next to a Chippendale's calendar if it ever was put on a shelf for sale. What he hoped people would compare it to were other calendars for charity, or the kind that showed fantastic images of far-off places to visit.

Once, when he was young, he and his family took a vacation to Canada. They had purchased a calendar of tourist spots all over the country. He looked forward to turning the calendar page each month so he could see what the next picture was. And he spent quite a bit of time dreaming of traveling to places like the Yukon, which offered one of the world's best views of the aurora borealis. The calendar showed an image of the northern lights that looked more like a wormhole taking passengers to distant locations across the universe. Many a clear night in the summer was spent looking up and wondering if life really did exist on other planets.

Not that he expected they'd sell so many calendars that bookstores and those mall kiosks would order any. It was too late in the year for that. But maybe if it did well enough, they could put together another calendar for next year and begin selling them in the summer at various locations around the state. Cody had ideas for new pictures should they decide to do another one next year.

But first he had to make sure that this year's calendar was done in taste and wouldn't shed a negative light on the town or his Christmas tree farm. So when he walked into the printer's shop and saw the look of horror on Sadie's face, he froze.

"What? What happened?" Cody couldn't imagine what had gone wrong. Fortunately, this was just the proof. It wasn't too late to fix it.

"Uh, I think we're going to need to have a talk with Jake." Sadie put the picture she had been holding facedown on the counter and looked away.

Within three strides, Cody was next to her. He picked up the picture and groaned. "No way. He didn't."

She nodded. "He did."

Todd, the printer, looked embarrassed. "I'm so sorry. Jake swore to me that this was what you wanted."

"Thank goodness it's not too late to make any changes." Cody tore up the picture and looked to Sadie. "Do you still have the images you wanted to use?"

"Yes, thankfully I kept a backup on a thumb drive in my purse." Sadie rummaged through her bag, pulled out the digital storage device, and handed it to Todd. "Next time when one person places an order, don't make any changes without talking to the actual customer first."

"I know, I'm sorry. I should have known Jake would do something so stupid." Todd put the calendar in his hands under the worktable.

"You didn't actually make any calendars besides the proof, did you?" Cody asked.

Red flamed up Todd's neck and cheeks. He scratched his neck, which only made the redness more pronounced. "Yeah, I made a few."

"I'm not paying for them. And I doubt any of the other men want to be associated with that trash." Cody still couldn't believe Jake had substituted a photo of himself half-naked on a bale of hay for the one that Sadie had approved. When did he have the photographer take the picture? Or did he do it himself?

Sadie shook her head. "You have to destroy all of those calendars. You can't even give one to Jake." She turned narrowed eyes back to Todd. "And who approved the proof so you could start printing? We spoke and you agreed I would be the only one who approved the calendar."

Todd hung his head. "I know, and I'm very sorry. You won't be charged for these. Jake came by about an hour ago and gave me the okay. He said he got the approval from you."

This was a small town and people were always helping others, but Todd had been here long enough to know better than to take Jake's word for anything. Especially when it was something as important as this.

"And he even put himself on the cover? Are you kidding me?" The cover of one of the calendars Todd had thrown under the worktable had just caught Cody's attention, and he almost gagged at the image. A part of him wanted to see if Jake had taken over the entire calendar. Knowing how self-absorbed the man was, it wouldn't surprise Cody one bit.

"I'll work on the new layout right away. It should be about an hour, maybe a little bit more, and I'll have the proof ready for you to sign off on." Todd put the thumb drive into his work computer, pulled up the layout images, and started working on the new proof right away.

"I'm gonna hang around town until you get the new proof. I don't trust Jake. Not even as far as I can throw him. That guy's slicker than a snake greased with Jake's hair pomade." Cody held the door open for Sadie to exit.

A chuckle escaped Sadie as she walked past Cody. "I have to agree with you. I never should have asked Jake to be in the calendar."

"Well, if we do another one, we can ask someone else. There are other cowboys in the area who would help out." Cody had wanted to get another one of his buddies in place of Jake, but Max wasn't around town when they were doing the photoshoot. He had thought getting Max to pose on a John Deere out in a field of hay would have been great. Not that there were any fields of hay right now, but some of the summer images were done using a green screen anyway, so it probably would have worked out nicely. Next year he'd work with Max and his schedule.

When Sadie received a text from Todd an hour later, the two of them headed back to the print shop with their coffees in hand. They had spent the past hour sitting inside the Frenchtown Roasting Company drinking coffee and chatting about the schedule for the week. They still had so much to do to prepare for the upcoming weekend.

With a sigh of relief, Sadie held out the calendar proof. "This is exactly what I was hoping to see." She turned it around and showed Cody the cover.

When Cody's grin touched his eyes, Sadie's lashes fluttered. The beauty in her eyes, along with the intensity of the green, sent shockwaves of delight through his entire being. He could have sworn he saw visions of sugar plums dancing around Sadie's head and he'd gone into Christmas nirvana. And over a woman, no less. He shook his head and focused on the cover. "I thought you were going to have the firemen on the cover."

With a saucy grin, Sadie shrugged one shoulder. "I had thought about it, but then I decided that since we'd sell the bulk of our calendars during the Christmas season, it made more sense to have Santa on the cover with all of the men standing behind him."

Cody looked back at the image in his hands. "But we weren't all there at the same time. How'd you get us all in one picture?" He rubbed the back of his neck and tried to remember how many were at his tree farm at the same time. There certainly weren't twelve models there all at once. And they never did a photo together with Santa in the red sleigh and all of the men standing around it with jingle bells on. "I never wore any bells, nor did I stand next to a sack of presents."

"That's right." Sadie dusted her nails on her chest. "I happen to be fairly decent at photo manipulation. I took pictures of each of you and placed them just right around Santa. We did take multiple pictures of Santa in his sleigh, so that was easy. And when he was here there were three other models, so the basic picture is with four of the twelve."

"Huh, did they put bells on for their picture?" Cody looked at each man, but couldn't tell that the bells were added post-production.

"Nope, that was an afterthought. Do you like it?" She turned her head so she could see the cover image.

Normally Cody wore a grumpy expression. Last year, he had been referred to as the Christmas Grinch by several of the kids who came out to the farm. So when he felt another smile spreading across his face, he was perplexed. How in the world did this woman make him smile so much? "I do. It's a fantastic picture. And made even better now that I know you created this from multiple pictures."

"It wasn't too difficult since each model had at least a dozen photos in front of a green screen, even those who were positioned in snow. If you remember, we still put everyone in the barn on the green screen." Sadie took the calendar from Cody and pointed out the various models who weren't really in the images on the paper. Only those who were shown in snow had been photographed in the snow. The rest were taken inside the barn in such a way that their images would turn out best once the background was inserted.

Cody was nervous as Sadie slowly turned the pages. He was the January model, but she skipped that month. Probably on purpose. He prayed his image came out alright. Since it was the first one of the year, his was almost as important as Santa in December.

He was more than impressed by how well, and how classy, all of the pictures turned out. Even the one of Jake, who wanted nothing more than to be half-naked in print, looked really good in his full set of clothing. If his mom was still alive, Cody would be proud to show this calendar to her. Shoot, he was going to have to put them up all over the tree farm to help sell them, and he had no qualms at all.

Well, none so far. Sadie still hadn't shown him his picture. "Okay, now how about showing me January? Or did you have to change out the model for January?" A tiny part of him hoped he wouldn't be there, but then if she had changed him out, why was he on the cover with the other guys?

Sadie turned serious eyes to Cody. "Now I don't want you to fret. It looks fantastic. And I think you were the best one for January."

"You're making me nervous, Sadie. What's wrong?" Cody gulped, and there were no traces of a smile on his face now. In fact, he felt the pulling of skin around his eyes and he focused on the calendar. Even his nostrils began to flare, something he hadn't done in quite a while.

"Don't worry, it's a wonderful photo and I can't wait to put this up at home." Sadie winked at Cody, but he didn't notice.

Sadie opened the first page, which was an introduction to the calendar and told the story of the Christmas tree farm. Then, when she began to turn the page to show him January, Cody's stomach dropped all the way to his boots.

"Ta-da!" Sadie opened to January and held it out for Cody to see. She was grinning from ear to ear.

Cody's mouth opened and his eyes widened. Then he began to stutter. "Wha, how?" He pointed to his picture. "Is that really me? Did you manipulate the picture?"

The tinkling sound of Sadie's giggle caused Cody's heart to pound even harder in his chest, something he didn't think was possible at that moment. "No, silly. That's really you. We cleaned up a few lines and edges, but you really do look like that when you're out by your trees."

"But I look so happy. Like I really belong there amongst the blue spruces." This image of Cody was of him trimming one of the taller blue spruce trees that he had held back from sale for the past couple of years. They kept a few marked for tall growth as they had a handful of commercial clients who wanted the larger trees for their office foyers. This was one of them. In fact, he had already sold this particular tree to the city of Missoula for next Christmas. The city manager was there the first weekend of pre-sales, and she saw this one and knew it would be perfect for their city Christmas display next year.

"Cody"—Sadie put a hand on his shoulder—"you really do belong amongst your trees. You look handsome and the epitome of a cowboy. I think we could even do a calendar of just you during the various seasons on your farm and it would sell very well."

Cody chuffed. "Yeah, right. Like anyone would want to buy a calendar of only me."

Under her breath, Sadie admitted, "I would."

He didn't know if he was meant to hear it, but he had. And his heart soared. Was she interested in him? Should he ask her out? But what about the business? If things went wonky between them, he'd lose her help. And saving the farm was more important than exploring whatever was happening between them at the moment. So, he did what most guys in his boots would: he pretended as though he hadn't heard her comment and he saved that bit of knowledge for himself. Something to ponder later, after he'd saved his farm.

Just then, a chime to the tune of "I Want a Hippopotamus for Christmas" sounded, starting both Cody and Sadie back to the present.

"Sorry, that's my phone. I better see if it's important." Sadie pulled her phone from her back pocket and looked at the screen. "Ugh." She hit deny and put the phone back in her pocket.

"What? Was it a telemarketer?" Cody chuckled. He hated those calls. Thankfully, his cell phone had recently started to note when a call might be spam. He figured that if it was important, they'd leave a message. And nine times out of ten it was either that his car's warranty was about to expire (his truck was way past warranty time), or he had won a vacation with a major hotel chain. He knew all of those were scams.

When she looked at Cody, Sadie's face showed a hint of hurt, or was it anger? He wasn't sure. But she closed up the emotion she was feeling, and he wondered who had tried to call her. It wasn't a spam call.

"It was nothing. Just an ex, that's all." She took the calendar over to Todd, who had been quietly watching them as they reviewed it. "I approve. Do you need me to sign the proof sheet?"

"Sure thing. But first, please read each and every word on all of the pages to make sure I didn't miss anything. Once you sign-off, I'll begin production in earnest. I need to start tonight if we're going to have a few hundred ready for this weekend." Todd handed her the proof sheet for sign-off.

Sadie took the sheet and the calendar before sitting down at a table in the corner. "Cody, you go on back to the farm. I 've got this covered." This time, her smile wasn't nearly as bright as before and he knew the situation with her ex wasn't a good one.

But then again, who really did have a good situation with an ex-boyfriend? They were always an ex for a reason, weren't they?

Chapter 12

The weekend came and Sadie couldn't believe how fast the calendars were flying off the shelves. They weren't cheap, either. A twenty-dollar calendar seemed like a high price to her, but Sadie knew they wouldn't make any significant profit if it was any lower.

It was only Saturday afternoon and they were almost sold out. This was a good sign. She was going to have to make sure Todd increased his production run this week. And maybe she could even get him to sell some at the shop. Although, any middleman would want a cut of sales, so that idea went out the window about as fast as it came.

The Channel 7 weather girl was coming this afternoon, and she would help to sell more calendars as well. Now that she thought of it, she'd need more calendars for tomorrow. After the weather report tonight, the tree farm would be overrun on Sunday with locals from as far away as Bozeman. Sadie pulled out her phone and called Todd.

She grinned when she put her phone away.

"What's made you smile like that?" Cody walked up and put his thumbs in his belt loops, then leaned back on the heels of his boots.

"Todd knew this was going to be this successful. He never stopped his run of calendars. Tomorrow morning he'll send out another three hundred calendars. And if you come close to selling out tomorrow, he'll start up first thing Monday morning with more and just keep going until we tell him to stop." Things were looking up for the farm. Now if all of these people coming out here to get the calendars and look at the various booths set up over the weekends turned into tree sales, Sadie knew that Cody would be able to save his family farm.

"Wow, that's fantastic. I can't believe it's going so well." Cody looked out at the carnival, which had set up a few kiddie rides and some game booths. It wasn't a lot, but it was enough to ensure that families would spend several hours each weekend at his tree lot. No one would want their trees until after Thanksgiving, but with the presale idea Sadie had come up with, he was already on track to sell more in person than he'd done since he had taken over the farm.

A feeling of accomplishment and satisfaction filled Sadie. She had promised Cody she'd help him in any way she could, but she'd never thought it would do this well. All she had to do now was wait for the weather girl to show up and do her thing, and then the tree lot would be overrun with families and singles looking to have fun on the weekends, and buy trees.

"Cody, are there any other tree farms that supply trees to Frenchtown?" Sadie hadn't been home for the Christmas season in a while. In fact, this would be her first full season since she'd left for college. There were two tree lots in town, if she remembered correctly, but she didn't know whose trees filled those lots.

The toe of Cody's boot rammed through a ball of snow at his feet. "I have one lot in town, and my competitor from up north has the other. There are families who only buy from him."

Sadie sensed a story here, but she wasn't going to pry. "When does he set up?"

"Both lots are up and running the weekend before Thanksgiving. We sell very few trees the first few days, but it's more about getting set up than selling trees. I do sell quite a few wreaths that opening weekend." His face lit up. "And we'll probably sell a lot more calendars then, too."

"Okay, how about I go and check out the competition opening weekend? I can see if they have anything we don't." Both lots did custom flocking, she knew that much. But she couldn't remember what else the other guy sold. Her family had always come to this tree farm for their trees. They wanted them as fresh as possible and always on December first, no matter what day of the week that fell on. If it was a Sunday, then they went after church. Any other day and they went in the evening after all the chores were done and the animals fed.

"The local diner wants to set up a booth to sell chowder and beef stew once we start selling trees. I think it'll be a huge hit." Cody had set up a few more booths during the week, and they'd sold out the minute they started running.

When Cody showed her the little booths he and Daniel had made during the week, Sadie couldn't help but smile. A feeling of home and hearth had settled over her the moment she saw the mini-barns. Cody had formed square booths with slanted roofs and then painted them red with white trim, just like his own family barn.

The two of them walked around the area holding the booths. Sadie pointed to the one where some of the ladies were selling quilts. "Looks like our quilting bee ladies are going to sell out for December even stars." They had a line around their little booth. Three walls were solid, while the front had a nice hole, big enough to look inside and see the stock that was available.

The ladies had also put up a few shelves on the outside of the booth to showcase a few of the smaller items they made. And on one part of the outside wall they pinned up a quilt sampler to show the level of detail and skill that went into their custom creations.

"I have to say, I'm surprised at how many people are out here buying up what all everyone is selling." Cody shook his head. "I mean, I knew people liked Christmas junk…"

"Hey, now." Sadie interrupted. "Don't go calling quality handmade products "junk", customers might hear you and leave."

He held his hands up. "Sorry, but for most men, it is ju…I mean…Christmas baubles." He chuckled and ducked out of the way when Sadie tried to lightly backhand him.

They both smiled at each other and continued on with their inspection of the various items being sold.

Sadie had made sure to make a list of vendors who wanted a booth in case they had time to make more. The support from the town, as well as from businesses across the state, was phenomenal. They also had a taco truck that would be out there every weekend from now until they stopped selling trees. "That's great. How would you feel about opening up the tree lot during the week?"

"Oh, we are open seven days a week starting the Friday before Thanksgiving," Cody said.

Sadie shook her head. "No, I mean now. How about we try being open from Thursday through Sunday? We've got so many people here now, it might be a good idea."

Some of the vendors would only be there Saturday and Sunday until the main opening. But if others could make it, then they might make a little more money.

A pensive look crossed Cody's face and he rubbed at his scraggly beard. "I don't know. I think with all of the new booths and extra services we have, we need the weekends to work out the kinks before the main event."

"But everything is going so well. What's there to work out?" Granted, Sadie didn't know all the ins and outs of running the farm and the tree lot, but surely it was already going smoothly, wasn't it?

"Ah, no." Before Cody could explain, an explosion went off and everything went dark. There were a few seconds of complete silence, then screams and cries of fear were heard all over. "This is why."

Sadie watched as Cody and his team pulled out lanterns and set them up. She went around and calmed a few kids and their parents, letting them know all was alright.

One father stopped Sadie. "What was that sound? It sounded like a bomb went off."

He wasn't the only one who thought that. Thankfully, this wasn't the first time Sadie had heard a main breaker burst. "It was only the electricity. We seem to have overdone it with the lights today. Nothing to worry about. We do have an extra line scheduled to be brought out this week."

When Sadie had suggested all the extra booths and opening up early, Cody had informed her that they'd need more power. He usually had the power company bring in a temporary line right before Thanksgiving. When he went to see about getting it brought in early this year, they were booked. So he wasn't scheduled to receive the extra power line until Tuesday.

"How will you get power restored tonight?" the father asked.

"I know Cody has a few generators. We won't get all of the lights back up, but we will have enough until the temporary line can be brought in." Now Sadie felt awful. It was her idea to go ahead and do all of this extra stuff. And the weather girl was due any moment. If they didn't have some power up and going, the report would be bleak for sure.

She made a beeline for the barn, where she knew the generators were stored. "Cody, how can I help?"

The cowboy didn't stop what he was doing. Instead of looking at her, he kept his eyes on the work before him. "Just help keep people calm. I'll have some lights back on soon. It's a good thing the ride operator brought in his own generators."

Sadie looked to the rides and noticed that a few of them already had lights on. They were prepared, she'd give them that. When she went back out to the people, most had already moved toward the carnival area. With a great sigh of relief, she noticed that only a few cars had left during the blackout. They could make this work. Although, she did worry about Sunday and how it would all work out. If the weather girl did a good piece on the tree farm, there would be an onslaught of visitors all day Sunday.

Could she get an electrician out here tonight to fix things? She looked around for Daniel, the foreman for the tree farm, and went to find him. She found him out behind the barn, putting a few cords together leading from the generator to the lights surrounding the booths. And she realized that Cody and Daniel were giving power to the vendors before they lit up the trees, or even the main house. They had prioritized the spots that needed power the most.

Realizing that Daniel was busy, she made a mental note to speak with him later. Then she went to look at the guests again. When she went out to the mini-midway, she noticed that the weather girl was there doing her weather report. She also had a copy of the calendar in her hand.

Standing behind the cameraman was also a news reporter. It looked as though Bianca had brought company. Sadie could only hope they would give a stellar report on the tree farm and the mini-carnival.

Once Bianca was done with the weather, she brought up the calendar and Sadie could tell she was talking animatedly about it. Then the news reporter—some guy Sadie didn't recognize—joined Bianca in front of the camera.

When a person stopped right next to Sadie, she almost jumped. She turned her head and breathed a sigh of relief. "You scared me."

"Who? Little ol' me?" Megan turned innocent, round eyes on Sadie and put a hand to her chest. "I'd never do that."

"Uh-huh. And you've never disarmed an assailant in ten seconds flat." Sadie knew for a fact that the woman had.

Megan was military through and through. And she was tough. Tougher than most men Sadie had come into contact with. Sadie had witnessed Megan throw a man twice her weight over her shoulder when he came up from behind and tried to put her in a choke hold. It was a demonstration for the single women in town a couple of months back, but still. Megan wasn't the type of woman a man would want to make angry.

Thankfully, it took a lot to make Megan angry. Or at least, that's what the tough-as-nails veteran had told Sadie after the self-defense class she'd taught last summer. She'd just shrugged and said, "When you've got it, you've got it."

Sadie had to laugh at that. Megan was honest, but also humble. While the woman had done a lot, she never let it get to her head. Which was what made her such a good friend. Sadie never liked women who thought too highly of themselves, or men for that matter.

Megan nodded to the television people. "Looks like you're gonna get a good report tonight. When that weasel Sam showed up, I thought for sure he'd say some negative things about this place." She whistled. "And when the power went out? I thought for sure he'd kill every good thing Bianca had to say."

Since Sadie didn't know the reporter, she had no clue what he might have said. All that mattered was what he was saying now. "I can't believe he likes the calendar and wants one for his office."

Megan chuckled. "He probably wishes he was a cowboy, or a fireman." She shrugged. "Or maybe when he was a kid he wanted to be one, or both."

"I'm just glad the carnival team had their own generators. I can't imagine the report would have been good if they didn't." Sadie bit her lower lip, trying hard to keep images of people screaming and fleeing out of her mind. If anyone had been hurt, they could have sued the tree farm. And that alone could have bankrupted Cody.

"Shh, listen. You can hear Sam's report. He's talking about the blackout." Megan put a finger to her lips.

Sadie's ears perked up and she listened with interest. At first it sounded like Sam was going to bad-mouth the farm, but then he explained how all of the employees had worked to calm the crowd and how fast the power came back up. "You know what I mean. We've all lost power in a winter storm and sat in the dark for hours, or all night."

Bianca joined in. "I know last year at Christmas when that blizzard came through, I was stuck in the studio almost all night long with very little power. The backup generators only gave enough light for those of us stuck inside to see where we were going." She shivered. "But tonight, power started coming back on very quickly. Quite impressive. I think we all can learn a thing or two about being prepared."

The news reporter nodded and smiled into the camera before signing off for the night.

"Do you think the station will use any sound-bites and put something on their website or social media accounts?" Megan grinned from ear to ear.

Excitement bubbled up as Sadie considered the segment. "I do think we'll see more. I need to find out what hashtag people are using and make sure we use it as well when discussing the events this year. I wonder if #BigSkyChristmas is available? I'll have to check that out tonight and see if we can use that going forward. Maybe put the word out to have people use it whenever they post about their time here."

"Ooooh, oooh." Megan bounced on her toes and waved her hands. "Maybe by next weekend I can have some of our guys put together some photo booths and put the hashtag and the name of the farm somewhere prominent, and encourage people to share pics from here."

Sadie turned to Megan with wide eyes and put a hand on her arm. "That's a fantastic idea. I don't know why I didn't think of it sooner." She began making mental notes of all the things she needed to do before the farm opened the next day.

At the top of her list was ensuring that she could use #BigSkyChristmas on all social media platforms.

Chapter 13

The electrical fiasco had kept Cody up most of the night ensuring that they had as much working as possible. Thank the good Lord he kept a supply of circuit breakers and knew how to replace them. This wasn't his first rodeo, thank you very much.

However, with all the drain on his power, he did need to ensure that the carnival used as much of their own power as possible. And he'd also have to use the generators for his outlying buildings. They weren't as big or as nice as the carnival's, but they'd do. He just had to get through today without any mishaps and then he'd breathe easier. On Tuesday the temporary power line would be brought in, and he'd have plenty of juice to light up everything just like a giant rodeo, or carnival.

And of course, he was running late this morning. If only he could find his other boot, he'd be golden. Well, he'd still need at least two pots of coffee before he could think straight, but that was just a matter of time. He'd wake up. If the coffee didn't do it, the cold air would. They'd had more snow overnight. Thankfully, he was almost done with the outside part of the job when the flurries began.

"Ahh, nutcracker!" Cody had just remembered where his other boot was, which meant he'd need a different pair today.

The dummy that he was last night—or rather, early this morning —took his boots off at the mudroom door and left one outside. It was caked with mud and dirty snow. He had planned to come back and get it to clean it off after he warmed up a bit, but he'd fallen asleep instead. Now he'd have to clean that boot and put it inside to warm up.

"The day already getting away from you, son?" Grandpops stood there in his flannel pajamas grinning like a fool with no teeth in.

"Ah!" Cody put a hand up. "Grandpops, how many times do I have to tell you, don't leave your room without your teeth. It's scary this early in the morning."

"Early, you say? Why, it's almost ten o'clock. That's late. What are you doing up here instead of outside gettin' ready for the day?"

"I was up until well past three in the morning making sure we had enough power everywhere to get through today. And now I have to go back to my room to get my old work boots." He turned around and headed back to his room.

Grandpops followed him. "Why'd ya gotta change your boots? Already messed 'em up?"

Cody shook his head. "No, I left one boot outside all night caked with mud and I'm sure it's frozen solid by now. I'll have to clean it up before I leave the house."

"Nah, I can do that. You run along. Get yerself some coffee, too. You're gonna need it if what I saw on social media this morning is true."

That stopped Cody cold in his tracks. He turned around and looked at his grandfather as though he'd grown two heads. "What do you mean, what you saw on social media?"

Most people his grandfather's age didn't even know the phrase "social media," let alone have one account. But not his grandpops. No siree, his grandfather had accounts across all platforms. Even the video-sharing ones. Who knew a man who couldn't remember to put his teeth in each morning knew how to take a video on his cell phone and upload it to the internet? And what's worse, he had more followers than Cody!

"That lady friend of yours, Sadie, she set me up yesterday with the accounts she wanted me to follow. And we started hashtagging the figgy pudding out of the internet!" An old man's wild cackle came from his grandpops, and Cody shuddered.

No one should have to see an old man in worn-out winter PJs with no teeth laugh like that. You'd think he was Jed Clampett. All he needed now was his shotgun and he'd make the perfect picture.

Cody ran a hand down his face and mumbled, "It's too early for this." Then he straightened up and resigned himself to what was coming. "So, what did you see this morning on social media?"

"Everyone's talking about our tree farm. They all want to come and get one of them there fancy calendars you guys made." Another cackle emanated from the Jed Clampett wannabe.

Maybe Cody should think about putting the shotgun away so his grandpops couldn't carry it around and scare the customers away. *The Beverly Hillbillies* was his favorite TV show. In fact, he still watched it whenever it came on any of their channels. And if it had been on recently, he was sure his grandpops would be hoisting his shotgun all over the place. Especially today.

"Really? So the news segment garnered a lot of positive attention?" Things were starting to look up now. Cody needed to grab his boots and get out there to make sure all was running smoothly before they opened at eleven.

Grandpops nodded. "Sure did. And the video of the power going out and everyone screaming has the internet wondering if our farm is haunted." Again, he cackled like a crazy old coot. "Say, we should do a haunted house theme next year and sell those pumpkins you were talking about. Maybe even a haunted maze."

"Not bad ideas, but this is Christmas. And if we don't make enough this Christmas, there won't be anywhere for us to hold a haunted-house-themed corn maze next year."

Cody went to his room and put on his older work boots. They tended to leak after about an hour, but by then his regular work boots should be warmed up enough to put on.

He prayed.

But when he finally made it outside with a large thermos full of hot coffee and a pastry in his mouth, he almost lost it. He had to walk around to the front of his house in order to see the end of the line. He didn't know how he hadn't heard all the cars and the people; there were hundreds in line, waiting for them to open. "Ah, jingle bells! This is going to be a very long day."

"You mean a very profitable day." The sultry female voice right behind him was enough to make him lose his pastry.

"Sadie. Good morning." He coughed and wiped the crumbs from his scruffy beard. One he hadn't had time to trim that morning.

"Can you believe it? We're the talk of the town right now, and the internet, too. People are all talking about coming out next weekend from as far away as the Dakotas, and even a few in California said they were coming." She rubbed her gloved hands together and grinned at him.

"But there aren't enough hotels in the area to handle that many people." Cody wasn't sure if he had the room to handle that many people. He'd have to ask the sheriff about crowd control and so many other things this week. He was on his way to getting a rotten headache, and they hadn't even opened for the day.

Now his toes were getting cold and his stomach was growling. A few bites of a day-old pastry wasn't nearly enough to get him going. He'd have to search out one of the food booths and see what they had.

"Oh, I brought you more of our huckleberry scones." Sadie handed him a little brown bag.

It was as though she was reading his mind. "Ah, bless you. I needed these today." He put a hand inside and grabbed the first scone he touched. He gobbled it up so fast that Sadie hadn't even finished what she was saying about social media numbers and bloggers picking it up and trending. Whatever all that meant. He really didn't care; all he cared about was that he didn't need to answer her as he ate his scone.

Then he picked up another one and took a bite. The pastry was flaky, but not like a croissant. As he continued to enjoy the sweet treat, Sadie's words finally struck a nerve. "Wait, what?" he asked.

"I think by next weekend we could easily see over five thousand people a day coming through here. We're gonna have to hire a parking crew and maybe even a shuttle service. Although, I think it would be best to use wagons and horses. Gives it a real down-home feel. Don't ya think?"

Now Cody wished he hadn't eaten anything; the food in his stomach was turning it rock hard. Why did he think the news segment would be a good idea? And why hadn't he thought of the pitfalls of being a success? This alone would bankrupt him. He didn't have the capital he needed to pay for all of these services. Most of his money wouldn't come in until the trees began leaving the farm. And speaking of trees, he and his team were gonna need to put in some seriously long hours cutting them down this week in order to start shipping them to the distant lots. The first of the trucks arrived this Friday to get a load, and they hadn't done anything other than tag the trees they were going to send on the first two trucks.

No expletive fit for a lady would do to stress how deeply he was in trouble.

"Cody? Cody, can you hear me?" A frown accompanied Sadie's voice.

"Huh? Yes, I'm here. Sorry, just thinking about how to handle all of this."

"Well, you don't have to worry. That's what I was trying to tell you when you tuned out. Did you hear my plan?" Her frown was replaced with the sort of smile an adult gave a child who was misbehaving, but in a cute way.

Great, now Sadie thought of Cody as a misbehaving small child. Well, at least he wouldn't have to worry about asking her out for the moment. "So, what was your plan again?"

"I'm glad you asked." She clapped her hands and stomped her feet like she was trying to warm up.

"Are you cold?"

Sadie waved a hand. "No, silly. I'm excited. You're going to save your tree farm this year and be around for a long time to come."

"Not unless I can get some help with crowd control and more food vendors by next weekend. Shoot, I don't even know if we'll be able to handle all of the customers today." Cody scratched his scruff and looked around. They had the taco truck and two coffee carts, thanks to Lottie for thinking ahead. He also had the pastries that Sadie had already brought over to the booth next to one of the coffee carts. And there was a hot dog truck the carnival folks had brought.

"The carnival guys. We can ask them to bring in more food trucks next week."

He continued to ignore Sadie as he thought of ways to handle all of the people. There was nothing he could do about today, but next week he could probably get plenty of food trucks here, and he'd have the power to handle them.

Something cold and wet hit Cody on the side of his face, bringing him out of his reverie. He looked around, expecting to see a group of kids running for their lives. The kids around here didn't call him the Christmas Grinch for nothing. As steam began to rise, he noticed Sadie standing a few feet away with her arms crossed over her chest.

"Will you please give me your attention? I have most of it sorted already. Including how to pay for it all." An imperious brow arched above one beautiful, stormy green eye.

A slow grin formed on Cody's face and he nodded. "Sorry, I got stuck in my head again. Nice aim, by the way."

She blew on her gloved fingers and polished them on her jacket. "I know. It helps growing up with siblings who like to have snowball fights."

"I knew there was a reason I wanted brothers."

"You can have mine. Malachi isn't so bad, when he's off at college. But Jackson…" She sighed and shook her head. "You'd think he was my dad and not my brother."

"Overbearing?" Cody had seen a smidgeon of what Jackson could be like. It didn't bother him. In fact, he'd inwardly chuckled when Jackson had given them a hard time about standing too close together.

"You have no idea." Her face fell when she looked out at the farm. "In fact, here he comes. Now be nice, he's going to help us out today."

He wasn't sure what she was talking about—Cody was always nice, wasn't he? —but he put a smile on his face and greeted Jackson when he approached. "Jackson, so good of you to come out and help."

Jackson grunted, but shook Cody's hand. "Someone has to bail my sister out." He turned his gaze to Sadie. "Looks like you bit off more than you can chew… again."

Sadie laughed. "This is a good thing. And not just for Cody, but for the town. Think of all the people who'll be coming through and spending their money here." She waited a moment before continuing. "We can even butcher a few pigs and put out the meat wagon you insisted on buying but have never once used."

That imperious arched brow of hers made another appearance. It seemed Cody wasn't the only one who brought out the feistiness in her. Although, from the look on Jackson's face, he didn't enjoy it like Cody did.

Which only made Cody smile. Jingle bells, what was going on? Cody couldn't remember smiling so much since...well, since his parents died. Now he smiled several times a day when Sadie was near. What was wrong with him?

Then what she said sparked a memory. "You have a food truck, don't you? I remember hearing something about it last year. Rumor was that you were going to do one of those fancy bacon trucks. But I don't remember seeing it at last year's Christmas carnival. Did I just miss it?"

Sadie smirked. "Nope. My pea-brained brother didn't think about what all was needed to stock a bacon truck. Food trucks aren't easy to manage, especially when you use pork. I've already got Dad working on how much pork we might need for next weekend, and Mom's working out the recipes. I was thinking bacon-wrapped Twinkies and Ding Dongs—those seem to go down well with carnival lovers. And we can do BLT sandwiches quite easily. Then we can also do Mom's famous pulled pork sandwiches."

Jackson interrupted. "What about bacon-topped mac 'n' cheese?"

"Oh, I vote for that one." Cody raised his hand.

"I second it." Daniel raised his hand. "Are we getting that today?" He rubbed his belly. "That sounds like just what this body needs to get all this work done today."

"Daniel, who's opening the gates?" Cody looked around; no one had been admitted to the grounds.

"That would be me. But since we have so many people out there, I wondered if we should set a limit on how many we let in?" The blasted cowboy grinned from ear to ear. He was enjoying this way too much.

"Why are you so happy?" Cody narrowed his eyes. "That pretty cowgirl from the Crooked Arrow hasn't finally agreed to go out with you, has she?"

Pink tinged Daniel's cheeks. "Well, she's here with two truckloads of guys to help out. These military guys are great with crowd control. Megan saw the news report and Jerod told her to round up as many volunteers as she could. So they brought almost a dozen hard workers. I told her we'd feed them today, and then later we could talk about some sort of payment once we had money coming in."

Sadie hit Cody's shoulder. "This was one of the ideas I was trying to tell you about when you freaked out over the success earlier."

"So, we don't have to pay those veterans today? They'll help us out with crowd control and parking and all of that?" Cody couldn't believe what he was hearing. He knew those men were worth any amount of payment Jerod, the ranch owner, deemed necessary, but he just didn't have any extra cash right now.

"Nope, Megan said they would want some sort of compensation going forward, but for today it's their weekly service hours." Daniel waved. "I gotta get going and unlock the gates. I just wanted to let ya know that we'll have a bunch of volunteers. And you'll need to find a way to fix them lunch and dinner." He walked away before Cody could answer.

"This is a lot to take in. But how am I going to feed them all today? I don't have enough food here for that." Cody thought about ordering pizza, but he doubted it would make it to him before others tried to claim it as their own. In a crowd like this, one didn't order delivery.

"I've got it covered for today," Sadie said. "My parents had plenty of meat in their freezer and they pulled it out last night. They'll bring over the ground beef patties and we can grill up burgers. I went by the store this morning and bought a ton of chips and soda as well as water bottles. So we should be fine for today. Next weekend, the workers will be fed from the family food truck."

Sadie really did have it all in hand.

Cody didn't know why he hadn't paid attention to her when she'd first told him all of this. He'd have to figure out a way to pay her back for everything she'd done for him already. "When I start getting cash in, I'll pay you and for family for the meals. Just let me know how much so I can cover it all."

She shook her head, and Jackson said, "No need, man. We all wanted to chip in and make sure you don't lose your family farm. That's what neighbors do, right?"

"But—" Cody blew out a sigh. He knew this was what neighbors did for each other. His family had always helped anyone who needed it over the year. And he always donated Christmas trees to families in need, anonymously of course. However, being on the other end of charity didn't feel right. Especially when he would have plenty of money if the traffic kept up like this through Christmas. "I need to do something to repay your hospitality."

Jackson grinned. "You can give us one of those ginormous"— he put his arms out as far as they would go—"Christmas trees for our house."

"Done." Cody chuckled and nodded his head. "Your whole family can have any tree they want, as long as it isn't already tagged for someone else. And maybe"—he turned to Sadie— "you can help me choose a tree for the Crooked Arrow Ranch? Just as a thank you for their help?"

"Of course. But I think you'll be paying them starting next week." She held up her hand. "They already agreed to wait to get paid until you started getting enough cash in to pay them. All of the guys over at the ranch want to help. You know, most of them have a strong desire to feel needed again. I've been to the ranch. Some of them won't be able to interact with the visitors yet, but most will. The quieter ones can help with the animals. In fact,

Jerod offered to bring out a couple of his wagons and horses to help act as a shuttle service so that people who park far out don't have to walk."

"Does he have sleighs? Or sleigh runners? I don't think regular wagons will do well in this snow." With the nightly snowfalls lately, even if Cody cleared a path for the horse-drawn wagons, they might not work well.

"He said he has it under control." Sadie went on to tell Cody about all the other ideas she had, and to inform him of the work his grandfather was doing on social media. "I swear, your grandfather is almost as good as Santa at getting the word out."

They both turned around when they heard a familiar voice and laugh walking behind them.

"Who's almost as good as me? Ho, ho, ho." Santa laughed and held his fake belly full of jelly, helping it to move along with his jovial laughter.

Sadie pointed to Cody. "His grandfather."

"Oh, yes. Joseph Makinaw has an unbelievable following. He even has more than I do." Mrs. Claus, dressed in her famous Christmas cape, touched her chest and smiled warmly at the group. "Any time I want to get anything out, I just let Joseph know and somehow everyone knows by the end of the day."

"That's my grandpops. Very social." Cody looked to the house and hoped his grandfather was putting on suitable attire for today, along with his teeth. The last thing they needed was a toothless grandpops scaring the little kids.

Mrs. Claus looked at Sadie, then to Cody.

Santa noticed the hint of a smile on her lips and the twinkle in her eye.

It seemed Mrs. Claus had another matchmaking scheme in mind.

Chapter 14

The big day was approaching: the tree farm would officially open for business the first Friday before Thanksgiving. They already had their big-top tent set up with an assortment of pre-cut trees ready for families to pick up and leave. The lot in town was sufficiently supplied with pre-cut trees, along with about a thousand calendars. And they used trimming from the trees to make more wreaths.

Several of the older ladies in town would man the wreath booth at the farm, like they used to do every year with Cody's mom. A week before the official opening, they would come in and take the trimmings and begin making fresh wreaths. They added various adornments such as ribbons, pinecones, and red berries. Each wreath was a little bit different, giving them a custom feel.

Cody knew the lot in town wouldn't sell that many calendars or wreaths during opening weekend, but they should do a lot of business throughout the season. Which would be wonderful for the profit margins. He had more calendars in reserve out at the tree farm, but he wasn't sure if he would be able to keep them all in stock. And every day the ladies would make more wreaths during the day, and some even took scraps home at night to make more before bed.

Pre-sales had done so well that Cody knew it was going to be a profitable year just in tree sales alone, not to mention all the other items they were going to sell, as well as the mini-carnival.

It truly was a Christmas miracle. Business had been off the charts since the news report and Grandpops' social media campaigns. And the old man had been at it night and day. He could be seen walking around the tree farm—and now the tree lot—taking mini-videos on his phone and sharing them all over the place.

Sadie couldn't have been happier with Cody's grandpops. The man was a marketing machine. And of course, Mrs. Claus had been tagging, liking, and sharing everything she had seen. Coupled with her own posts, the tree lot was trending, big time. Whatever that meant.

Sure, Cody knew about social media thanks to his grandpops, but he wasn't much for it and certainly didn't know the lingo. Although, Sadie was schooling him on everything from TikToking to friend requesting, and all sorts of sub-groups for Christmas events. And everyone wondered why Cody stayed clear of social media? Anyone who had any following on those sites had to spend a minimum of eight hours a day on them.

It was no wonder Cody's grandfather always had his face in his phone, and most days forgot about putting in his teeth until Cody told him to. The old coot was so consumed with his social media campaign, he couldn't be bothered with anything else. Except for going outside toothless, Cody didn't mind an absent-minded old man wandering about the place in his own little world. It kind of added an air of mystique to the place, which only brought out more visitors.

In fact, one social media post that Sadie showed him just that morning had him laughing so hard, he had to bend over to get air.

When Sadie came to the farm that day—the day before the official opening, when they'd have the trees ready to go—she was beaming. "Look at what your grandfather has done." She shoved her phone into Cody's face.

He had to pull it back a bit to see it clearly, for she had shoved it so close that it was practically touching his nose. "What is this?"

Sadie tsk'd and then sighed. "It's just the best marketing video ever! I wish I would have thought of this sooner."

"My grandpops made a killer video?" Cody rubbed his chin and watched a video of some kid talking about a strange old man who hovered around the place, almost like a specter. "This isn't Grandpops. It's some kid who's been here recently."

"Shush, keep watching."

A grimace made its way across Cody's face once the video turned to his grandpops wandering aimlessly. The man was dressed properly, thank the good Lord. But he was without a hat and his hair was all over the place, like he'd been putting his hands through it all day long. Or he'd literally just rolled out of bed. Not like the teens today who sculpted a messy look.

A creepy music played in the background. "Is that *The Adams Family* theme song?"

Sadie laughed. "Yes, isn't it great?"

Cody's large hand rubbed across his face and he shook his head. "I think it might be time for my grandfather to enter a special home." But Cody didn't really want his grandpops to leave him. However, if his grandfather was senile, he wouldn't be able to help the poor man.

"No, you're not getting it, Cody. This is golden."

"I guess I'm not. I'm seeing my poor grandpops looking like a senile old man, meandering and walking into trees, then saying 'excuse me' to trees. He's treating them like people." Cody sighed. "I knew my grandfather was getting old, but didn't realize he was becoming senile, or..." He waved his hand. "Is this dementia?"

When the light tinkling of Sadie's giggle hit Cody's ears, he looked up. "This isn't funny. It's quite serious."

"No, he's not senile or demented. He's brilliant." Patient, beautiful green eyes looked upon Cody.

"I don't get it. How can an old man looking like a fool be brilliant?" Would this generation of social media craziness ever make sense to Cody? He didn't think it would.

Sadie pursed her lips. "Think of it as a marketing ploy. If you saw a commercial of an old man you didn't know acting like this"—she pointed to the video as it replayed on her phone's screen—"wouldn't you be curious to know more?"

Cody thought about it for a moment. "No, I think I'd feel bad for him and his family and hope they could get him the help he needed."

"You're thinking about this from your standpoint. Think of it from that kid's perspective."

Finally, after more back and forth, Cody started to see the entertainment value of an old man walking around talking to trees and staring into his phone. When Sadie said that he resembled more of a fun-house type character, Cody started to understand. His grandpops was *acting* the part of an oddity, like the old carnivals when they had the bearded lady or the shark babies. It was something odd that grabbed people's attention and brought them in to see it for themselves.

"So, you think that my grandpops trending on this TikTok thing is going to bring in families?" Cody wasn't too sure about that, but he'd see how it all went before passing judgment. Just as long as his grandfather was safe and treated well.

"I do."

And Sadie proved correct in her assessment.

As the first day of tree sales went on, Cody heard more and more kids talking about the famous, crazy old man. The first time he heard it, Cody had been incensed that people talked about his grandpops in that manner. But when his grandpops came out acting the part again for all to see, this time with his shirt untucked and wild eyes, Cody realized his grandfather was acting the thespian. People clapped and cheered, and he began to overhear the kids begging to come back again next weekend.

It was as though his tree farm had become an amusement park. While they weren't charging for parking, they were charging for the wagon rides to and from people's cars. And that money was split between all of the Crooked Arrow ranch hands that helped out. Sadie really had come through for him, big time. He owed her a lot.

If things kept going like this, he'd have no trouble getting through to next year, when he could do even bigger things and bring more people out, beginning in September with his new fall festival and pumpkin patch. Come January, he'd have to write out a lot of notes for how he would put next year's events together. Maybe he could even rent a bus and bring people in from town—for a larger fee, of course.

Then all sorts of ideas flooded his mind about expanding and buying the neighbor's land to plant more trees as well as a larger pumpkin patch if the next few years worked as he dreamed.

"So, what do you think of the first full day of tree sales and the carnival?" Sadie asked as they closed up the farm later that night.

"I'm exhausted, but excited at the same time. I think I'll need a good cup of calming tea to help get me to sleep. Care to join me?" Cody had already sent his grandpops in for the night since the man was obviously exhausted with his play-acting all day long. They were going to have to limit the performances in order to ensure his grandfather didn't drain himself.

Cody would never forgive himself if his grandpops got sick from working too hard to save the tree farm. Or worse, died from exhaustion.

Sadie nodded. "I'd love to join you. Thank you." She followed him inside, feeling the long day creep up on her as well.

When Sadie sat down, Cody noticed her shoulders sag and her eyes droop. "Hey, maybe I should make you some coffee to help get you home? I don't want you to fall asleep at the wheel."

She waved away his concern. "Don't worry about me. I'll be fine. It's only a ten-minute drive this time of night." Her family farm wasn't too far from his, and if she drove fast, she'd get home alright.

"Well, be sure to get plenty of sleep. You're gonna need it tomorrow." Today was Friday, and Sadie was needed there for opening day, but they had already discussed her going to their competition and seeing what they had at the other lot in town. The nearest tree farm was too far away to truly be considered his competition. No, he'd only worry about the lot in town.

"I'll be sure to get plenty of sleep. Then I'll stop in at the tree lots in town. I'll check them both out before coming to the ranch, so don't expect me until after lunch."

"Why check out both?" It was too early to worry about how his lot was doing. Wasn't it?

"Well, after I see the Jingle Jangle Christmas Trees lot, I want to check yours out and compare the two."

"I guess that makes sense. Be sure to ask Adam if he needs any supplies. If he's starting to run low on anything I'll need to get the boys working on restocking right away." Cody knew he had supplied his lot in town with everything they'd need for opening weekend, but with all of the hype, one never knew.

Sadie finished her tea and was about to leave after they completed their discussion of what would be done the next day when Cody coughed and stood up. "Uh, I'll walk you out to your truck."

"Thank you, but it's not necessary. I was able to get a spot right out front." Then she stopped and looked at him. "What about tomorrow? Maybe we should designate a few spots in front of your house for those who'll be staying late? I'd hate to have to walk down the road to the parking lot." Cody had a spot of land about four hundred yards away, but it was only accessible via the main road. That was the largest of the parking areas besides what was already next to the barns. And those spots went fast.

"I'll have Daniel put up a few reserved signs out front of the house and then again by his trailer. You're right—I don't want any ladies who work late to have to walk across that dark road late at night." Cody thought about how best to handle the parking for the employees and vendors, something he hadn't really considered.

"Maybe you could keep a wagon here and then take people out to their cars at night when everything's all closed up? Or drive them in your truck?" Sadie offered the use of her truck as well when she stayed late, but Cody declined her help.

"I'll ensure that everyone gets to their vehicles safely at night." Cody walked Sadie to her truck, ignoring her protests. "Sadie, I wanted to talk to you alone."

Her eyes widened and her brows rose above her bangs. "Oh?"

"I don't know..." Cody stammered. "Uh, would you... I mean..." He took his hat off and ran his hands through his hair. Then thought better of it. "Never mind. It was a crazy idea."

When he turned to leave, Sadie reached out her hand and touched his bicep. "What? If you want to ask me something, please do." A softness entered her eyes, and he relaxed.

"We've been getting along quite well, and you've helped me out so much already." Cody looked down at his snow-covered boots. "Would you go to dinner with me on Monday night?" They usually didn't have much of a crowd at the tree farm on Mondays in November, and he knew his crew could handle a slow night without him and Sadie, at least for now. Once December came, it would be crazy every night of the week.

Sadie bit her lower lip and hesitated. "Do you mean...as a date?"

"Uh, yes. If you'd like. If not, I understand. We can just have dinner as friends." Cody was feeling flustered. He'd really messed this up. He wanted a date, not dinner as friends. How could he get her to go out with him on a date if he couldn't even ask her properly?

She sucked in a breath. "I'd like that. It's a date." Then she turned and opened her car door, leaving Cody standing there surprised, but happy.

Chapter 15

On Sunday morning, Sadie rose with the sun and prepared to attend the early service at her church. She was grateful that during November and December they had two worship services, thanks to the influx of people who came to town for this season, most of whom needed to work Sunday afternoons. Hence an early service was offered. Since Sunday school was offered at ten in the morning, followed by the usual worship service at eleven, during the Christmas season her church offered a service at eight in the morning. Most of the out-of-towners, or ranch hands who worked the special events, came to that one.

The early service was something new this year. Her pastor was a forward-thinker, and after the news report about the tree farm he announced an early service for those who would have to work Sundays. The first time she attended this service was the previous weekend, and she was surprised by how many attended. Not all of them were working, either. Some were early risers and wanted to start their day worshipping the Lord.

In the bulletin this week, they had printed a verse from Proverbs:

A merry heart doeth good like a medicine. But a broken spirit drieth the bones. – Prov 17:22

The day's sermon was focused on positive thinking, which was something Sadie had been reading a lot about in her morning devotionals. It was funny how God worked sometimes. She would study a topic for a week, sometimes more, and then the Sunday sermon would be a deeper dive into the topic she had been reading on every day. And the sermon usually put it all into perspective for her.

This week was no different.

It was easy to get overworked and forget about all of her blessings. It was also easy to look at the negative instead of the positive all around her. Yesterday had been a tough day. A few older teens had showed up to the tree farm looking for Joseph. They had seen his videos online and decided it would be funny to harass the poor old man.

Cody had focused on how poorly his grandpops had been treated and ordered his grandfather to stay indoors the rest of the day. He was also grumpy and short-tempered all day. The teens had been kicked out and asked to never return.

The memory from the previous night bothered her and she needed to put it behind her. Sadie prayed that Cody would, as well.

At first, Sadie was so happy that the social-media influencer from Idaho had shown up. However, it hadn't taken long to see that was a mistake.

"Sadie, I don't like those guys hounding my grandpops. And I certainly don't want to stand around and watch as customers video the embarrassing situation they've put my grandpops in." Cody walked toward the kids before she could even say something.

He grabbed both boys the scruff of their jackets and yanked them away from his grandfather. "Didn't your mommas teach you how to behave? Treating the elderly like some sideshow isn't right."

A crowd had formed around them and most had started clapping when Cody went off on the boys. They only have him a hard look. One boy spat in his face while the other wiggled away.

Both yelled obscenities at Cody, and his grandfather. Thankfully, a few of the guys from the Crooked Arrow were close enough and came to drag the sons of nutcrackers away.

Sadie and Cody both followed Sam and Skeeter who held each boy by the arm.

"You both are banned for life. I don't want to see you here again. If I do, I'll call the Sheriff." Cody crossed his arms over his chest and glared at the boys who flipped everyone off.

Unbeknownst to Sadie, the social-media influencer had gotten it all on video. When she shared it, it went viral almost immediately.

Sadie battled with herself over whether or not she should show Cody. Even after a few hours of sleep, she wasn't sure showing it to Cody was the right thing.

Of course, the majority of the comments supported Joseph and shamed the kids for their actions. But Cody didn't see it the same way. All he saw was his grandfather being made fun of and over a million views.

Cody shoved the phone back into Sadie's hands. "I don't want to see anything like that again. Do you hear me? My grandpops isn't a clown to be made fun of."

Sadie saw the tears forming in the corner of Cody's eyes. She felt for the man, she did. But these things happened. Shoot, she'd seen plenty of videos where the elderly were walking down the street and mean-spirited kids who really needed to be on the naughty list had said or done awful things. Those videos usually received a ton of views, and most everyone supported the people who had been made fun of, but kids still did it. It seemed they thought the more negative comments they received, the better they did.

Cody turned his back on her and didn't speak to her again the rest of the night.

That hurt.

She wasn't even sure if they were still on for their date on Monday night. And she felt horrible. Poor Joseph, the sweet man who only wanted to help his grandson save the family tree farm, had been harangued and even pushed around a few times by the mean-spirited boys. Thank the good Lord he wasn't injured. But still, the man had to feel awful.

But after the sermon about focusing on the positive and not letting the harsh day break her spirit, she felt recharged and ready to tackle the day. Yesterday had been a good day for sales. In fact, now that she thought about it, once the video of Joseph went online they seemed to be flooded with well-wishers and people who weren't stingy with their pocketbooks.

As Sadie drove out to the tree farm, she decided to put a happy face on. She'd go check on Joseph and then finally look at social media. She hadn't wanted to look at anything after the incident, so she wasn't really sure how it was all going. She did hear from some of the visitors that it was trending, but she was too afraid to check for herself.

The first person she saw after parking in her reserved spot was Joseph Makinaw, the man himself.

"Joseph, how are you doing today?" Sadie gave him a great big smile, choosing to think positive and show a happy face. She knew from past experience that if you let yourself get down, it would be more difficult to get back up. Staying positive really was the best way to avoid the doldrums, or a small bout of depression.

"Sadie, my dear. So good to see you." Joseph rubbed his hand and lowered his voice. "Have you seen the latest videos and comments?" Thankfully, his grin showed he had his teeth in this morning. Sadly, she had seen him a few times without his dentures, and she hated the way his lips turned in on his gums when he tried to smile.

"Not yet." A sheepish smile appeared on her face, and her shoulders hunched. "I must admit, I was a bit afraid to look. But after this morning's sermon, I decided not to cower in fear and look once I got here."

Joseph smiled. "I showed Cody how to watch the sermon online this morning. He's not the most tech-savvy. I thought your generation was supposed to be computer literate while mine wasn't." He laughed. "But it seems we've swapped roles, at least where modern-day technology is concerned."

Sadie had to agree. She'd noticed how illiterate Cody was when it came to computers and smart phones. "So, did it improve his mood?" She wasn't sure what to expect when she saw Cody today, so she hoped the sermon had spoken to the man.

Joseph nodded. "It did. And he even listened when I told him how yesterday was a good thing."

Sadie quirked a brow. She wouldn't say it was good how Joseph was treated, but maybe some good could come out of the bad. That was how God worked sometimes.

"I know." He waved a hand in front of his face. "But if you'd seen the social media reports, you'd know it was good. I think we're gonna have a surge in visitors this week." Joseph cackled, then coughed.

"Oh Joseph, are you alright?" Concern for the old man's health took over, and she led him back inside the house, not wanting to keep him out in the cold weather any longer than necessary. On her way to the tree farm she'd heard that more snow was on its way. The afternoon should see more snowfall, but at least it wasn't going to be a blizzard, just light flakes dropping all afternoon.

"I'm fine, don't worry about me. I just got a bit too excited." He took them both to the kitchen, where he offered Sadie some coffee. "Cody's got me working inside the barn today, getting more of those wooden ornaments cut and holes drilled so folks can hang them on their trees."

"Thanks, I could use some. And that's a great use of your time. I think we're going to sell out on the ornament kits." She sat down at the kitchen table.

Joseph grinned and waggled his brows. "And a few of those church ladies insisted on helping me put the ornaments in the clear plastic bags."

She chuckled. "I see. And I take it that it was the single church ladies who insisted on helping a poor, old man?" Sadie waggled her brows in response.

"Oh, I don't know." Joseph coughed to cover his grin, but Sadie saw it.

When older people got together, it was so cute. Sadie hoped that even though Joseph was getting up there in age, he could at least have a lady friend to spend time with. Now, to only ensure that Joseph was being treated as fairly online as he was in person.

Sadie looked through the social media accounts on her phone. Wonder of wonders, everyone was supporting Joseph and telling those teen boys they needed to learn some manners. A few harsh things were also said about the boys and how their mothers had raised them, but Sadie decided she didn't need to read any of the hateful messages. She chose to focus on the positive and supportive messages.

One thing she had learned from being a marketing manager was to avoid the negative social posts as much as possible. It did no good to interact with the negative ninnies and only served to make her feel awful if she read too many of those sorts of posts.

"What do you think, will we see an influx today? Or will they wait for Friday?" With Thanksgiving coming, Joseph wasn't sure how the week would go.

Sadie turned a sweet smile on the old man. "Joseph, I think we're going to see a great deal of families coming to show their support for you all week long. And next weekend, well…" She fanned herself even though it was a bit chilly in the kitchen. "I believe we'll need to make sure we have plenty of help on hand, as well as food."

"Why will we need food?" Cody asked when he entered the kitchen with a scowl on his face.

So he was back to being a grumpy Grinch. Sadie would have to ensure he saw the positive aspect of yesterday instead of the negative. "Because the internet is all agog to support your grandfather. I expect we'll see a record-breaking number of people coming through your gates all week long. And next weekend—the first official weekend of the Christmas season—will bring so many people, lines will be out the gates all day long and the food trucks are sure to run out of food." Sadie had been to events where the food trucks ran out food to serve, and it wasn't a pretty sight. "I think we'll need to make sure all of the area food trucks are invited to participate next weekend."

Cody rubbed his neck. "Next weekend also marks the start of the town's Christmas festivities. I don't want to take away from what they're doing. Most of the money raised goes toward the new college fund as well as disadvantaged youth."

Sadie remembered the events from her past visits to town at Christmas, but she had forgotten about the new scholarship fund Chloe and Lottie had started last Christmas for the town's high school graduates who went on to universities around the state. "Right, we don't want to interfere. So what do you suggest?"

Cody rubbed the stubble on his cheek and looked out the kitchen window at the tree farm coming alive. "Maybe we can donate one dollar from each tree sale at the lot to help the local kids going to college?"

Sadie blinked, then widened her eyes. "Why, that's a wonderful idea. It will keep a lot of people in town over the weekends when the regular town events take place. Maybe your grandfather will even come visit the tree lot in town on Saturdays throughout the season. That would help a lot."

"But what about here?" Joseph asked. "Would funneling most people into town hurt the sales here?"

Sadie thought for a moment, then shook her head. "I don't think we'll have any trouble continuing with the sort of numbers we're seeing. Not everyone who comes to town will know anything about the town's fundraisers."

"There you have it." Joseph nodded and exited the house, leaving Cody and Sadie gaping at him.

"Uh, I guess that means Joseph's on board with visiting the town's tree lot each Saturday moving forward?" Sadie wasn't sure if Joseph had meant to say more but didn't, or if he thought they could read his mind.

Cody chuckled and shook his head. "I think this has all gotten to my grandpops just a little bit."

Unsure exactly what was going on, Sadie finished her coffee before saying another word. "So, how are you feeling today?"

Cody winced when he looked at the unsure expression on Sadie's face. "Look, I'm sorry how I acted last night. You gotta understand, my grandpops means everything to me. He's more important than the farm." He sighed. "But I was wrong in taking my frustrations about how those boys treated my grandfather out on you. I know you were almost as upset as I was."

"You're darn tootin' I was. I was about to grab one of those foam candy canes lining the fence and beat them over the head. Those, those... Well, let's just say it took God to calm me down. I wanted nothing more than to bend them over my knee and give them a good spanking. Surely they've never been punished a day in their lives for doing something bad." It wasn't that Sadie thought all kids should be spanked, but sometimes a slap on the backside was exactly what a bad kid needed.

"Get behind me. If I ever see those boys again, I'll pull out the belt that my parents used when I was a kid. I've got plenty of sheds to take them to." He winked at Sadie to indicate that he wouldn't really spank another man's kids. "Although, if I knew their dads, I'd be sure to share a piece of my mind with them."

Sadie chuckled. "Okay, let's move on to something more pleasant."

"Like what?"

"Like calendar sales numbers." Sadie grinned and waggled her eyebrows.

Chapter 16

Tonight was the night Cody was to take Sadie out for dinner, and Cody had to admit to himself that he was nervous. Every time he thought about the dinner, his hands shook. The only thing distracting him was the customers who continued to pile in to his tree farm in droves. He was conflicted over the events of the other day when his grandpops was basically accosted by those teens. But on the other hand, it served to bring in more people who asked after his grandpops.

Mondays were supposed to be slow days, but if anything, this Monday was turning out to be one of his busiest days to date. He had to call Jerod over at the Crooked Arrow and ask if he had any more men he could send to help out. The taco truck had to send someone into town to get more supplies, as they began to run out of food just past lunchtime.

When Daniel came up smiling, Cody frowned. "I don't know why you're so happy. This place is a madhouse."

"Which is exactly why I'm smiling. We're killing it on sales, and it isn't even Thanksgiving." Daniel put his hands on his hips, still grinning.

Which only caused Cody to frown deeper. He was beginning to understand why the Grinch was so unhappy with Christmas. The constant hustle and bustle of the crowds, the demanding shoppers, and the lack of food was giving him a headache. "I don't think I'll be able to go on my date tonight."

"Bite your tongue, Cody. You're most certainly taking that pretty cowgirl out to dinner." Daniel narrowed his eyes when Cody looked to the food trucks. "No, no you don't. I see what you're thinking."

Cody turned back with feigned innocence. "What are you talking about?"

With his finger pointed right at Cody's face, Daniel narrowed his eyes. "You will not take Sadie to dinner at a food truck for your first date. You will take her into town for dinner at the steakhouse. I know your grandpops and your father taught you better manners when it came to taking a lady out for your first date."

Cody held up his hands. "Don't worry. I think I'm going to reschedule our date so I can take her out and not spend the evening worrying about this place. I never had any intention of serving her food from a truck for our first date."

"Then why were you looking at the food trucks?"

With a sigh, Cody looked around at the tree farm and all the people coming and going. "For the first time, I've got a large amount of customers who are buying up everything in sight. I can't afford to leave this and go have a nice time while everyone else is out here working so hard to save my"—Cody put a hand to his chest— "family farm."

"I understand, but you need this time with Sadie. And she needs a night away from all this. You aren't even paying her." Daniel scoffed.

"I offered to pay her and she refused. She said she'd only accept trees for her family as payment." Cody knew that wasn't really payment. Giving someone one of his Christmas trees was something he did when someone did a favor for him. What Sadie was doing was so much more than a favor. It went way above and beyond. And Daniel was right, she deserved a nice night out.

"She's too nice for the likes of you."

Cody furrowed his brows. "Wait, I thought you were interested in Megan?"

Daniel's head popped back. "What? No, I'm not. I was thinking that if you didn't take Sadie out, I would."

A slow grin crept across Cody's face. "Then why have I seen you and Megan going on sleigh rides together?"

"What do you mean? I took her out on the sleigh once so she could see the grounds. That's all." Daniel grumbled and toed his boot in the snow.

"Uh-huh, and you've got a bridge to sell me?" Cody was finally beginning to relax and enjoy himself. If he wasn't mistaken, his best friend and farm foreman was really into the pretty counselor from the wounded warrior ranch. He'd have to find a way to ensure that the two of them spent more time together.

"I think we have a lot of work to do." Daniel left Cody smirking and went back to helping customers pick the perfect tree for their house.

Once Daniel was no longer in sight, Cody thought about what his friend had said. He really shouldn't cancel on Sadie. To be honest, he was looking forward to spending time alone with her. Well, as alone as one can get in a restaurant. They'd spent a lot of time together since late October, but it wasn't the same as a date, and even he knew that much. But, he was also nervous.

Although Cody would never admit this to anyone, not even to Daniel, he was out of practice when it came to dates. He couldn't even remember the last date he went on. How in the world was he supposed to act in a completely different environment than what the two of them had been accustomed to sharing?

Instead of talking about the farm and all the different aspects of expanding his business, they'd be expected to discuss their personal lives, which Cody did not have. All he did was take care of the farm and his grandpops.

So when the appointed hour arrived, he was surprised to see Sadie still working at his tree farm instead of already gone home to get ready for their date. "Sadie? What are you still doing here?"

"Cody." She smiled at him. "I still have plenty of time to get ready. Don't I?" She looked at her watch and screeched. "Oh my little drummer boy. I'm so sorry, time got away from me today. It's been non-stop craziness." She looked down at herself and sighed.

Cody watched as her head tilted down, and he too looked at what she was wearing. It wasn't bad, just a bit dirty. It looked to Cody as though she had been helping cut down trees, or load them into the wagons and vehicles. "How much time do you need?" It had been so long since he'd had a girlfriend, Cody had no clue how much time a woman took to get ready.

When Sadie looked to Cody, her eyes were starting to tear up. "I'm so sorry, I've ruined our night."

Cody took two steps closer. "Hey, don't worry about it. The only reason I'm ready is because Daniel practically shoved me into the shower." He chuckled and watched as she wiped the tears away from her eyes. None had dropped yet, so he was grateful for one good thing.

Wasn't that what yesterday's sermon was about? Finding the positive in all situations? The positive here was that she didn't actually cry. But also that she enjoyed working at his tree farm. She must have liked it if time got away from her so easily.

Would suggesting they get something from the food truck and go back inside his house and eat there be alright? Or would she balk at the idea?

"Look, it's already getting late and we're so busy tonight." She bit the inside of her cheek. "Would you mind rescheduling for tomorrow night?"

He grinned and felt his heart grow two sizes in that moment. Sadie was more concerned with the success of his tree farm than with their date. But as he thought about it, he wondered if that meant she wasn't all that into him.

Sadie put her hand up. "Maybe tonight we could just grab something from one of the trucks and go somewhere away from everyone else to eat it? I know it's not really a date, but it could be a nice time to talk about something other than the tree farm."

"You took the words right out of my mouth. How about we get something from the taco truck and head inside my house? It's warm and quiet in there."

Sadie's shoulders relaxed and she let out a sigh of relief. "Thank you, that would be fantastic." She held up one hand and inspected her fingers, which weren't in a glove. "I think I could really use some warmth right now."

"What happened to your gloves?" Cody took her hands and rubbed them between his gloved ones, then blew on her fingers to warm them up.

Her dirty blond hair glided around her shoulders as she shook her head. "I think I took them off earlier when I was helping with the trees. But I don't know where I put them. I can't find them anywhere."

"Here"—Cody took his gloves off— "use mine until we get inside. I'm sure I have several pairs of women's gloves that have been left here over the years." Once she had his gloves on, he took her hand and led them to the taco truck.

Chapter 17

Sadie couldn't have been more embarrassed than she was the previous night. Tonight, she had her alarm set for the correct time. She wasn't about to lose out on a chance to have her real date with the handsome cowboy.

Sure, the previous night's taco dinner was nice, and the conversation even better than she'd expected, but it wasn't like a real date. It felt more like two friends or coworkers grabbing a bite to eat after work.

It wasn't like she needed romance to feel like it was a date, but she did need a different place than where they worked. Even going to a food-truck event not on the tree lot's grounds could have been a fun date. So it wasn't the food truck that made it feel like a non-date.

Or was it that they had tried dating too late after meeting one another? Could two friends become more? There were a ton of songs, books, and movies about friends-to-lovers. No, that wasn't it. But there was something missing from their time last night.

As she went over the evening in her mind, it came to her. The dinner felt like a work thing because every time they spoke about something outside of work, it always circled back to work, or the tree farm. Did they have anything in common besides wanting to save the Christmas tree farm? Or was the lack of spark last night because they truly were just friends and coworkers?

That was what she was thinking about when her phone's alarm went off. Sadie pulled her wrist up to see the time and stopped what she was doing. "Sorry Daniel, I've gotta go if I'm going to be ready in time."

"So, are you really going on a date with Cody?" Daniel asked.

Butterflies rattled around in her stomach, and she nodded. "Yup, and I'm going to try and look my best for him. I still feel bad about last night."

"Nah, you shouldn't feel bad. Those things happen." Daniel picked up the twine and the Christmas tree that was waiting to be tied to the car only a few feet away.

"Don't work too hard. You've gotta make sure you're in top shape for your date with Megan." Sadie was joking with Daniel. As far as she knew, they weren't going on a date any time soon. The pair of them seemed more like the Hatfields and McCoys than Romeo and Juliet. All day long, every time she saw Megan and Daniel talking, it was more like fighting. She only hoped the two realized how much they liked one another before someone said or did something they couldn't take back. If things worked with Cody, Sadie hoped Daniel and Megan would double date with them.

Once Sadie arrived at the steakhouse, she parked and got out, scanning the parking lot for Cody's truck. It should be easy to find as most of the trucks at the restaurant were newer models. Cody drove an older Ford truck that was in desperate need of a new paint job. The old midnight-blue paint had begun flaking off, showing the gray primer.

Just as she was about to pull out her phone and call the late man, an older truck pulled into the lot. She grinned when Cody stepped out wearing fresh clothes and wet hair.

"Sorry, I hope you haven't been waiting long. Why didn't you go inside to wait where it's warmer?" Cody put his hat on his head and walked to her. He had parked right next to her truck.

"I only just arrived myself," Sadie admitted.

"Whew, then I'm not alone in running late?" he asked.

"What caused you to be behind tonight?" Sadie tilted her head and scanned the cowboy from head to toe. He was wearing dark-blue denim jeans that were clean but not new, along with an older button-up blue chambray shirt under his black winter jacket.

"Work stuff." He took her hand and led her to the door. "What do you say we don't discuss work tonight?"

She grinned. "I say yes."

After they were seated, Sadie picked up the menu and glanced over it. Not wanting to take too long in making up her mind, she had actually looked at the menu online Sunday night before turning her light out. And she had chosen what she wanted then. But in order to keep Cody from guessing what she'd done, she perused the menu and stopped when she found the item she wanted.

Trying to appear calm and relaxed, which she was anything but, Sadie asked, "So, do you know what you want?"

Cody turned warm eyes on her and took a deep breath. "Yes, I do."

Sadie's belly felt funny and she wondered if *she* was what he wanted. Heat zoomed through her veins and she felt her face flush. "Good, so do I."

The two of them continued to stare at each other without a word until the waiter came to take their orders.

Cody started when the waiter addressed him first. He motioned to Sadie to order before him, as any gentleman would.

"So, what do we talk about if we aren't going to discuss work?" Sadie asked when the waiter had left.

"I must admit, I'm not really sure. It seems the only thing we have in common is the tree farm." Cody winced.

But Sadie knew they had more than that in common. And besides, weren't couples' differences what made them so unique? Her parents were total opposites, and yet they always had something to discuss. Plus, her mom had told her once that thanks to her dad, she had found new and exciting activities to enjoy, some she even loved.

"Hmm, I'd have to say that's not totally true." Sadie smirked and took a drink of her water as she waited for her Diet Coke to arrive.

Cody put his forearms on the table and looked into Sadie's eyes. "Okay, then what else do we have in common?"

"We both love Christmas. And a holiday isn't work." She wanted him to know that just because he owned a Christmas tree farm, it didn't mean the entire holiday was his job. He may help people and families prepare for the holiday, but the holiday itself wasn't his to work. In fact, tree lots were always closed on Christmas Day.

He held his hands up in surrender. "Okay, okay. We can discuss Christmas. What are your favorite parts of the holiday?"

"I love the entire season." Sadie grinned. "I'm one of those who listens to Christmas music before Thanksgiving." She looked around and leaned in as though what she was about to say was top secret. "And I normally decorate the weekend before Thanksgiving, so that come the Friday after Thanksgiving I can go out and do Black Friday shopping." She sat back in her chair and crossed her arms, almost in a *there, take that* sort of gesture.

Cody slowly nodded his head. "I can see that. So, is your house decorated already?"

Sadie frowned. "I wasn't able to decorate this past weekend because I have a taskmaster of a boss." She tried hard to keep from grinning. She even pursed her lips, but she knew her eyes were twinkling and the edges were starting to crinkle, so she let loose and the smile took over. "I decorated almost ten days early this year."

Shock was evident on Cody's face from the wide eyes and mouth opened in an O. "Really? Why so early?"

"Because that pushy boss of mine wouldn't give me any time off. And I seriously doubt I'll be able to do the Black Friday shopping this year, either. Or at least, not like I normally do." Sadie was alright with having to limit herself to Wal-Mart first thing in the morning and doing the rest online before heading into the tree farm. She knew from her own research that Friday was going to be crazy at both the lot and the farm.

"Well, maybe you should tell your overbearing boss that you want to come in late on Friday. Then you should have time to get a lot done." Cody grinned.

"Hmm, I might do that when I go into work tomorrow. Since, you know, I'm not allowed to discuss work tonight." She winked and smiled up at the waiter when he brought her the drink.

"Well, as your date I do appreciate keeping the work talk to a minimum since I don't really know much about what you do." He returned her cheeky wink and took a sip of his root beer.

Conversation flowed from there, and the two enjoyed a delicious meal of steak, potatoes, and asparagus.

On the way out, Cody asked, "Of the events the town does, which one is your favorite?"

"Oh, that's tough. Whenever I've been home for the holidays I've always done them all."

"Really?" Cody's brow furrowed and his nose wrinkled. "You don't find it to be too much? I mean, every weekend and a few nights during the week they have various things going on, from Thanksgiving dinner on Saturday all the way to New Year's Eve."

Sadie glanced at him sideways. "How many of the town's activities have you done?"

"Ah, not many. I do the community Thanksgiving dinner on Saturday, and then try to get to one of the other events each year. I try to shake it up and not do the same thing every year."

"Then you haven't really experienced the Christmas season. You see it from the perspective of a Christmas tree farm owner. You work every day, I bet, and never take a day off until Christmas Day?" Until that moment, Sadie hadn't really thought about how Cody and his family celebrated the season.

"I do the Christmas Eve candlelight service most years. So I guess I do one event regularly. Although, to be honest I haven't done it every year. There have been times I was too tired to drive into town. And last year, Grandpops was sick so we stayed in."

"Do you work all day because you have to, or is it because you don't really care to do the events all season long?" When they planned the events at the tree farm, Cody seemed interested in them, and he was adamant about not interfering with the town's events. So she thought he had enjoyed them on a regular basis. But maybe he just didn't want to steal any thunder from Frenchtown's own celebration?

Cody took her hand and walked slowly to his truck. "When I was a kid, my mom took me to most of the events, and my dad would choose two events he wanted to attend." He looked out over the parking lot and seemed lost in his memories.

Sadie noticed his eyes had gone watery. While she wanted to know what he was thinking, she also knew that he would tell her what was going on when he was ready. She may not know him very well, but she did know him well enough to know he wasn't the sort to overly share.

"I guess when I was in college, I thought I'd do the same thing. Work all the time at Christmas and choose two events to take my kids to." Cody shrugged. "I don't have any kids, so why attend the events designed for families? I'd just stand out like a sore thumb."

"No Cody, you wouldn't." Sadie paused a moment to sort her feelings. "The town's events are for everyone, not just families. I'm single with no kids and I go to as many as I possibly can." For a moment, she wondered if he didn't go because it brought back painful memories. She knew he had lost his parents while he was in college and he had to quit to come back and take over the farm.

"Whenever I do attend, all I notice are families." He narrowed his eyes. "I guess I just see the kids and assume they're there with their parents, so it's all families."

She squeezed his hand, but didn't let go when they stopped on the passenger side of the truck. "Are you coming to the community Thanksgiving dinner on Saturday?"

He nodded. "Yeah, Grandpops would tan my hide if I didn't take him." Cody chuckled. "I swear, he's more sociable than a cheerleader."

Sadie laughed. "You got that right. He knows just about everyone in town. How does he do that?"

"He was born and raised here. He's never moved away. The man never even went to college."

"Well, that's not surprising. Most people from his generation didn't go to college if they lived on a farm." Sadie had seen more and more of the kids recently going away to college and then coming home to help out on the family ranch or farm, thanks to so many local colleges offering degrees in specialized farming or ranching fields nowadays. She even knew of one kid who was off studying the geology behind the underground water reservoirs in Montana and Wyoming.

"You know…" Sadie said the last word long and slow. "If you got out and about more in town, and met more people, you could be just as sociable as your grandpops when you're his age."

"Now you're just making things up. You know good and well I don't have his sunny disposition." Cody arched a brow down at Sadie. "I know the town's kids call me Mr. Grinch behind my back."

"You weren't like that as a kid."

"You didn't know me as a kid," Cody countered.

"Actually, I did. We used to always get our trees from your farm. And I'd see you with the families on the farm. You even helped me out a few times." She wasn't about to say she even noticed him after she hit puberty and started thinking about him as a cute cowboy. That would be weird.

Cody took a step back, and when he did her hand fell out of his. Then he looked at her—really looked hard at her. Memories began to float to the surface. Images of a cute little girl who wore pigtails and had blond hair that was so light, she looked like she belonged in the Nordic region instead of Montana. Now she had beautiful dirty blond hair that she wore down her back. "I do think I remember you now. What happened to your white hair?"

Sadie slapped his arm. "It wasn't white. It was just very blond. And I grew out of it, thank you very much." She sounded a bit peeved with him, but she was joking. What she really felt was an overwhelming sense of emotion that she couldn't name. He had remembered her. Cody was popular as a kid and three years older to boot. How could he remember a little girl?

"Hey, no hitting." Cody took her hand and pulled her closer.

She didn't realize how hard he'd pulled, and when she flew into his chest she lost her breath. Not from the impact of her body against his, but from the nearness of her lips to his. She licked her lips as her entire being trembled from the anticipation of that first kiss.

When she noticed Cody's eyes turning black, he was looking at her lips. Her breath hitched and her eyelashes fluttered in preparation for when his lips touched hers and she would close her eyes. In that moment, there was nothing else around them. All sounds disappeared, and there was nothing in her vision but his face. She felt his breath on her lips as he inched toward her, and the moment she closed her eyes the world exploded with noise.

First, she heard the sound of metal on metal.

Then she felt the hard ground as Cody pushed her back and he fell on top of her.

Finally, the world crashed back into focus and she heard a horn blaring and people yelling.

"What? What happened?"

"Ahhhh, Je… Jingle bells." Cody had almost said something he really shouldn't ever say.

Sadie's eyes opened wide and she turned her head and winced. "Ow." She brought her hand up to the back of her head, and when she pulled it away there was blood on her fingers.

"Sadie?" Cody jumped up immediately and pulled her to him. Instead of kissing her like she had wanted, he moved his hands gingerly along the back of her head. "Where all does it hurt?"

For a moment she had lost all sense of feeling. Now, with the adrenaline rush almost over, pain was beginning to make its way back in. Sadie moved her arms; they were sore, but nothing big. When she tried to step away from Cody, she winced and reached down to her left leg.

Cody's eyes followed her movement and he saw the blood already seeping down her pant leg. "Thank goodness you weren't wearing a dress."

Sadie chuckled. "Not in snowy weather. Not even for a first date with Cody Makinaw. Sorry, but if you thought you might be getting a girly-girl, you're going to be disappointed. I rarely wear dresses."

"That's what I like about you." He grinned and then winced when he looked back at her leg. "Can you walk?"

Sadie went to put pressure on her left leg, but couldn't. She barely held back a yowl.

"Sorry." Cody picked her up in his arms and took her to the entrance of the restaurant while he waited for the emergency vehicles. When he sat next to her, he looked out at his truck and sighed. "I've had that truck since it was new. It was a graduation present from my parents."

"What happened? One moment we were, uh…" Sadie felt the heat in her cheeks and put her hands to her face.

Sad eyes looked at Sadie. "I'm sorry. This date did not end the way I had hoped."

She took his hand and intertwined her fingers with his. "It's alright. You didn't cause this accident." Sadie looked back at the truck for the first time and winced. "Do you think those people are alright?"

A crowd had gathered around the small truck that rammed into the bed of Cody's Ford. Neither of them had a good view of what was going on.

"I hope so. Maybe we should pray for them?" Cody looked to Sadie for confirmation.

Before she could answer, they both heard sirens in the distance.

"Sounds like help is on the way."

The door behind them opened and the manager of the restaurant came out. He looked at them in horror and put a hand over his mouth when he saw the blood on her leg. "Come inside and wait. Please. I'll get some towels to clean you and blankets."

A waitress came back with everything the manager promised, plus two large to-go cups of hot cocoa.

"Thank you," Sadie breathed out as she took in the scent of the hot chocolate.

Cody took the blanket from the waitress and wrapped it around Sadie as they sat on the long bench along the waiting area wall.

When a police officer came in, he tipped his hat at them. "Ma'am, sir. Were you involved in the accident outside?"

Chapter 18

"**W**ell, that didn't go as I had hoped." Cody sat down on the sofa in the living room where his grandpops sat.

Joseph looked his grandson up and down. "What happened to you? Why are you home so late?"

"A man hit a patch of black ice and collided with my truck while Sadie and I stood next to it in the parking lot. Thank goodness he wasn't going very fast." Cody put his head in his hands. The stress of the evening was beginning to wane, and he was starting to feel his own bumps and bruises.

Joseph sat up and looked upon his grandson, taking in the dirt and cuts along his hands as well as the blood on his clothes. "What happened to you? What about Sadie? Is she alright?"

Cody nodded. "We fell to the ground, but nothing really hit us. Well, except for the ground. She's very sore and needed stitches in her thigh. Something in the parking lot cut her open. Thankfully it wasn't too deep and the doctor said it was just five stitches. But she's to stay down for a few days of rest."

"And the other car?"

"The driver is fine. His airbags deployed and he's no worse for the wear. We would have been fine, too, if I hadn't been shoved forward from the momentum of my truck moving." The images of the scene flittered through his mind, and he shook his head in an attempt to dislodge them. That was something he didn't want to see ever again.

"And your truck?" Joseph knew how much that old truck meant to Cody.

"In the shop. Sadie's dad came to get us from the hospital where the ambulance took us. So, we're out of a vehicle for now." Cody wasn't sure how long it would take, but he doubted the insurance company would scrap the truck. It was old and not worth much, but if they could repair it, he'd be very happy to keep driving it.

"Maybe Daniel will loan you his truck when you need to go town? And he can take us in Saturday night for the Thanksgiving dinner?" Joseph stood up and went to sit next to his grandson on the sofa.

"I'll ask him tomorrow, but it's late and we need to get to bed. Do you have any Epsom salt? I think I'd like to soak in it before heading to bed." The doctor had told Cody he should soak daily for the next few days, as it would help his muscles recover from the event.

When he stood, he understood what the doctor meant. While he wasn't truly injured, he had clenched just about every muscle in his body when the truck hit him. And while it was true his fall had been cushioned by Sadie's body beneath him, he'd had enough wits about himself to use his arms to catch the brunt of his weight. Now his muscles were screaming at him to do something. The doctor offered to write a prescription for muscle relaxers, but he'd refused. Anyone who worked on a farm or ranch kept Epsom salt on hand for tough days. While this was a bit more than a tough day, he'd take two Tylenol and call it good.

Normally Cody's alarm went off at five in the morning. He needed to get up and make sure the few animals he had were fed and watered, then he'd walk around the grounds to see if anything needed to be done, like replacing lightbulbs that may have gone out overnight or picking up any trash that might have blown in. Most mornings he needed to get his snow-blower out and clean the paths before anyone showed up.

But that morning, his alarm never went off. "Grandpops!" It was almost ten in the morning and he doubted anyone would have done his morning chores, and the tree farm was due to open in just over an hour.

When his grandfather didn't answer him, Cody knew. "That sneaky, no good, ungrateful old coot!" He got dressed as quickly as he could and ran to the kitchen. The old man wasn't inside drinking his second pot of coffee like he normally did at this time of day.

Dressed for the cold, Cody left the warmth of the kitchen and his coffee behind. He was on a mission to find to the old man and discover why he'd turned off his alarm. But when Cody walked outside, he had expected to find the new snow covering everything. It had snowed again last night; when he was driven home by Sadie's dad, there was snow falling.

After his Epsom salt soak, he'd looked outside and saw it was really coming down. So why were there neat piles of snow alongside the walkways?

Cody knew his grandpops couldn't have done the snowplowing himself, and the blower was too heavy for him to carry at his age. "The animals." He took off for the barn, hoping to find his grandfather in there taking care of the beasts.

When he looked inside, all was quiet and the horses were munching on the last remnants of their breakfast. And his grandfather was nowhere in sight. "He wouldn't be out with the trees, would he?"

Cody turned to head out and felt a twinge in his lower back. "Ahh, crushed candy canes." That was sorta how he felt at that moment. Cody had to stop and take a breath, but he couldn't breathe in deep as the muscles all along his back began to spasm. Maybe he should have taken that prescription after all?

Slowly, he stood up and began to turn when he heard the barn door opening behind him.

"Cody, what're you doing up? Didn't you get my note?" Grandpops frowned as he walked toward the hurting cowboy. "You should get back inside and rest today."

"I can't, there's too much to do. Or at least, I thought there was." Cody scratched his hatless head and remembered in his haste he had left his Stetson on the peg in the mudroom. "Who did all this work?"

"Jerod heard about the accident and his men came out early to help. They got the pathways all cleared and salted. A few of them also fed the animals and cleaned the stalls. I was just out with Jerod himself going through the public areas ensuring all was in tip-top shape." Grandpops walked up to Cody and grabbed his earlobe. "Come on, you're headed back inside, now."

Cody felt like he did when he was only nine years old and he let one of the horses out by accident. He hadn't meant to leave the gate open, but he wanted to take an apple to the horse. However, he was told he couldn't go in the stall unless an adult was with him. His grandpops had discovered him hiding and grabbed his earlobe, like he did now, and hauled him inside for a lecture and punishment. He hoped he was too old for that treatment now.

But apparently he wasn't.

"Cody, you need to learn to accept assistance when you're injured. And my boy, you are injured." Joseph let go of his ear before they left the barn, but walked by his side until they reached the house.

He interrupted, "Grandpops, I'm not injured, just sore. I can work. And this season is too important for me to be sidelined."

"Knock it off, Cody. I may be old, but I can still throw you over my knee and give you a whooping." Joseph pointed his finger into Cody's chest.

Cody rubbed at the spot his grandfather had just been poking at. It hurt. Which surprised Cody, as he hadn't thought the old man had that much strength left in him. Or was it just because his muscles were sore from last night?

"Grandpops, I wasn't the one who fell on the hard ground or had to get stitches…"

Joseph interrupted Cody. "Now see here." He put a hand in the air to stop Cody from trying to interrupt him again. "You will sit your sorry backside down on the sofa and enjoy a day of rest. We've got this covered."

The fight left Cody as a wave of pain mixed with exhaustion flooded his body. He walked over to the sofa and sat down. As he did, another wave of pain went through his back.

Joseph put a bottle of Tylenol in front of his face. Cody grabbed it and held it while he watched his grandpops walk back into the kitchen. When he returned, he had a cup of coffee fixed just the way Cody like it, as well as a cup and a small jug with water in it. "Here ya go. Now there's no need to get up any time soon. Just sit back and watch some Christmas movies or something."

Cody grumbled under his breath, but he did as his grandfather told him.

"Now son, you'll only be down for a day or two. It isn't the end of the world." Joseph shook his head and left the room.

For an old man, he had a lot of energy this morning. Cody shook his head and after taking two Tylenol, he grabbed the remote sitting on the coffee table and turned on the TV. He grinned when he found an old John Wayne western. When he was a kid, he used to watch these with his grandpops. Turned out, that station was doing a marathon of old westerns. So he was nicely entertained all day. He'd never admit it, but he also took a few naps right on the couch.

Later in the day, Daniel came in and grinned at his friend. "So, how does it feel to laze about all day?"

"Pft." Cody gave Daniel the stink eye. "I'm forced to stay on this couch. It wasn't my choice."

"I know, I know. Your grandpops told me you got up and came outside all mad." Daniel chuckled. "But he's right, you do need to spend the day on the couch. And do yourself a favor."

"What's that? Get a new foreman?" Now it was Cody's turn to grin.

"Ha, ha, so funny. No, sleep in tomorrow as well. We've got tomorrow's morning chores covered. If you sleep in and feel fine when you wake up, I'm sure your drill sergeant of a grandfather will be fine to let you work. Just as long as you take it easy."

"Has Grandpops been regaling everyone with his war stories?" Cody's grandfather had served in the Army right after World War II. He had been too young to join for the war, but even after, it was tough.

"He and Jerod have been swapping stories. Even a few of the guys from the ranch who rarely talk were joining in. Megan says it's good for them to share their experiences." Daniel tilted his head. "So don't go messing this up. Think of it as helping those guys get the type of treatment they need."

Cody was surprised that Daniel and Megan had been talking so much lately. "Megan says, huh? I thought you two didn't get along?"

"Well, I had to look elsewhere for a date when you up and asked Sadie out." Daniel winked.

Cody knew his friend was never interested in Sadie; he'd only been teasing him. "So, when can Sadie and I double date with you and Megan?"

Daniel rocked back on his heels and looked down at the ground. "Uh, I don't think we're there yet. Maybe next year."

If there was one thing Cody knew, it was when to leave talk about a girl alone. Daniel would tell him about Megan when he was good and ready. Until then, he didn't mind not knowing, just as long as he could keep on teasing his best friend. "Or, maybe never?" He grinned at his friend.

"You must be feeling better. I swear, you need to stop grinning. The kids are gonna stop calling you Mr. Grinch if you don't knock it off."

Cody narrowed his eyes and stared Daniel down just like the Grinch would. "I don't think I'll ever lose my title." He pointed out the door. "Now get out there and get back to work, you lazy, ungrateful, mangy dog."

Daniel laughed and put his hand out to high-five him. Cody left him hanging. "Alright, I see how it is. Stay the Grinch. But I'm not going to tell you about Sadie."

Cody jumped up and grabbed his friend by the arm. He had tried calling Sadie twice already to see how she was, but her phone kept going to voicemail. "How is she?"

"Sore, but fine. However, her phone's toast. It seems it fell out of her purse when you pushed her to the ground…"

"I didn't push her on purpose. The truck forced me into her," Cody grumbled. That was the one part of the night he knew he was guilty for. And it gutted him, knowing that his body forcing her to the ground was what caused her leg injury.

Daniel held his hands up in a gesture of surrender. "Hey now, I'm not judging. But her phone ended up falling out and smashing to pieces when your truck tire ran it over."

He couldn't afford to replace her phone, and he knew it. Cody sat down and covered his face. "Nutcracker. How am I going to replace her phone?"

"You don't have anything to worry about. The other guy was at fault and his insurance will be paying out. Since she wasn't inside your truck, your insurance isn't responsible for anything but fixing your truck. All medical bills will be covered by the other guy, and he has great insurance." Daniel ran a hand over his chin. "In fact, I'm going to call my insurance guy and see what my insurance covers and make sure I've got good insurance, not the bottom-of-the-barrel coverage."

Cody nodded. After his parents died in their car during a blizzard, his grandpops had them both look up their insurance coverage and increase it. Higher insurance coverage wouldn't have saved his parents, but it would help cover injuries and the expenses of someone dying. Who knew calling a coroner out was so expensive? Thankfully, their insurance covered everything, including the cost to total out the car. It had swerved off the road in a blizzard and lay in the ditch overnight. If they had been found sooner, they might have survived their injuries. Injuries that would have cost a lot of money and been covered by a higher insurance policy.

"At least that's one problem solved." The memories of his parents' death had come and gone all day. They didn't slide on black ice, but it was still a snowstorm that cost them their lives. The situation was enough to remember everything he and his grandpops went through fifteen years ago.

Turning his thoughts back to Sadie, Cody asked, "How long is she down for? Can she walk today?"

Daniel shrugged. "I didn't talk to her. This afternoon, Megan went over to see how she was doing. It sounded like Sadie was really well, but she wouldn't be in to work for a while."

"I'm not worried about her coming in to work, I'm worried about her recovering in time to enjoy all of the activities the town does for Christmas. This is her favorite time of the year."

Daniel lightly patted his friend's shoulder. "Don't worry. Her parents are taking good care of her and she's going to be just fine."

"Do you have a number I can call her at?" Cody knew his friend was being honest, but he still wanted to talk to her. It was stupid, but he had to know for himself how she was doing. Plus, he had more questions. Questions that Daniel didn't think to ask.

When Daniel left, the first thing Cody did was call Sadie. When she answered the phone he let out the breath he didn't realize he was holding. "Sadie, thank goodness. How are you doing?"

"Cody, hey there. Sorry I didn't call you. There have been people coming to visit all day, and tons of phone calls. Every time I tried to call you, someone was either ringing the doorbell or calling on the house phone."

Sadie's voice calmed Cody's nerves. She sounded like her normal self, which was such a relief. It was one thing to hear from a third or fourth party that someone you cared about was fine, but it was totally different when you could hear their voice for yourself and confirm the truth of it all.

"Have you been able to rest today?" The doctor had given very specific instructions for Sadie to rest for the next few days. Cody hoped that all of this attention wasn't keeping her from it.

"I took one nap. Mom screened calls and visitors for me while I napped for almost an hour. In fact, I just got up and was walking by the phone when you called." Sadie lowered her voice. "I'm not really supposed to be answering the phone. My parents said they would take care of it all, but I was hoping it was you."

Relief dripped from Cody's shoulders. "I'm so sorry about your cell phone. Do you know how long it will be before you can get it replaced?"

"Hopefully tomorrow. I think I'm going to get my mom to take me to the store and then just submit the receipt to that guy's insurance company. My mom spoke to them and they said they'd pay up to eight hundred for a new phone."

She sounded chipper. Cody figured it was because she had just woken up from a nap.

"But enough about me. How are you doing?"

"I'm alright. Sore, but that's it. My grandpops is making me stay inside on the couch today." Cody relayed the morning's events to her, and Sadie laughed. Knowing she was able to laugh helped him to relax even more. If she had been in a lot of pain still, she wouldn't laugh or sound so good. He wished he could drive over and see her.

"What have you been watching?"

They spoke about daytime TV and old movies. Then, when Sadie noticed that *Miracle on 49th Street* was on their local channel, she suggested they watch it over the phone together. "It's almost like being in the room together."

Cody disagreed. "I'd much rather you be here on the couch next to me. But since neither of us can go anywhere right now, I'll take it." He changed the channel on his remote and sat back to watch an old black-and-white Christmas movie.

When it was over, Cody could hear the sniffling over the line, but thought better of commenting. "Now when I hear a bell, I'm gonna think an angel is getting his wings."

Chapter 19

Thanksgiving Day came and went without much fanfare. Sadie had to stay home, per her mother's instructions. Then on Friday, she went out to get a new phone and was exhausted when they returned. Using crutches wasn't easy. She ended up taking a two-hour nap, which only worried her mother. So, her mother ordered her to stay home for a few more days.

"Mom, I'm going out on Saturday night for the community Thanksgiving dinner. I'm not going to miss it." Her father agreed with her, and together they overrode Silvia McKinley's mother-hen attitude.

Since Sadie had slept in on Black Friday, and the effort it took to get her a new phone had zapped her of all energy, she was stuck inside ordering her Christmas presents online later in the day. "Ugh," Sadie complained to Cody Friday night. "I hate online ordering. You never know if the product is as good as they claim it is."

"But it's so much easier than going into those crazy shops. One year, Daniel came back from shopping with his mom and he had a black eye." Cody had never liked going out on Black Friday, or any day that weekend, for shopping. "Since the advent of online shopping, that's all I've done."

"Yeah, it can be great, but what about when you need to return something? Some places ship from out of the country." Sadie had learned the hard way not to buy gifts from Friendster; most of those ads came from China. And the cost to return something wasn't worth it.

"That's why I only buy from local stores. That way if I need to, I can return it in-store." Cody had an entire system he had worked out over the years, which he explained to Sadie.

"But I love to see the Christmas Crazy Ladies on Black Friday. It's always such fun." Sadie knew she couldn't go out; her stitches weren't even out yet. There was no way she'd be able to fight her way into the best lines and stay up on her feet. So, she shopped online.

Early the next morning, when she and Cody were chatting on the phone, she admitted it was simpler to buy online. "I'll have to inspect the gifts when they arrive and make sure they're the right ones, and they aren't the broken or leftover items from the sales this weekend."

Both of them chuckled.

"Cody?"

"Yeah?"

"Are you going to the Thanksgiving dinner tonight?" Because Sadie hadn't seen him since the accident, she missed him and wanted him to sit by her at the dinner.

"Wild horses couldn't keep me away." His voice took on a husky quality that sent chills down Sadie's spine.

She had to bite her tongue to keep from asking if she'd finally get that kiss they had almost shared before being practically mowed down by his truck. Instead, she asked, "Would you and your grandpops like to join me and my family?"

"I thought you'd never ask."

When it was time to leave for dinner, Sadie was just as nervous as she was for their first official date. The only thing that might spoil the night was her ex. Wesley had called and texted all day. Somehow he'd found out about her accident and felt he had to speak with her right away. She continued to ignore him and hoped he'd get the message. When he hadn't messaged in a few hours, she breathed a sigh of relief.

She did debate with herself whether she should talk to him. But after remembering how he'd ghosted her when she lost her job, he didn't deserve to talk to her. Sadie had decided that if he called again, she was going to block his number. There was no reason to talk to him again. Her life was in Frenchtown now. Sure, she would make the occasional trip back to Seattle for the few clients she had there, but with Zoom, there really wasn't a need to meet in person very often.

So when she dressed for the town's annual Thanksgiving meal, she only thought of Cody when she put on a dress. Well, that and the fact that jeans rubbed against her stitches, making them very uncomfortable to wear. A flowing skirt would be much more comfortable in this situation.

The look on Cody's face when she entered the community center was priceless. He stood there with his mouth open so wide, she thought the lower half of his face might fall to the ground. For the first time she wasn't using the crutches, but she did have a cane. And as she walked to Cody, her smile only grew.

Cody stood there, not moving an inch, and was going to enjoy this night.

"Wow. I mean, whoa. Uh…" Cody stammered, and didn't seem to be able to get his thoughts out.

Warmth spread through Sadie's entire being as she realized Cody was speechless over her. She knew if she played her cards right, she'd be getting that goodnight kiss tonight. Now to make sure her parents didn't hover too much. She'd need some alone time with the cowboy if he was going to make his move.

"You look very handsome yourself, cowboy." Sadie winked and gave him a hug.

"I love that dress. But I thought you didn't wear dresses?" Cody seemed to have gotten his brainbox working again.

"Well, I thought a dress was warranted tonight." She wasn't about to admit the real reason.

Sadly, her mom didn't have any qualms about spilling the beans.

Mrs. McKinley greeted Cody. "I'm glad to see you walking around just fine."

"Thank you, ma'am. It's been a rough few days, but I'm sure nothing like what Sadie's gone through."

"You've got that right. The only reason she's in a dress is because of her stitches. She can't wear jeans until they take them out." Mrs. McKinley put an arm around her daughter.

Then her dad got in on the game. "She's been in baggy sweatpants all week. I'm just glad to see her dressed in something besides black or gray."

"Gee, thanks." Sadie turned stone-cold eyes on her parents. "Why don't you go and get my plate for me? Cody and I will get seats at the table for us all."

Her parents tittered and acted as though they'd never seen their daughter date anyone. They both had silly grins on their faces, and Mrs. McKinley pinched her daughter's cheek.

Then Mr. McKinley looked at Cody. "This is my baby girl. You better treat her nice."

"Dad!" Sadie put a hand over mouth to keep from yelling anything else.

Boone McKinley, who wasn't as tall as Cody, put his hands up in the air in surrender. "I'm just looking out for you, sweetie."

Sadie turned her back on her parents, mortified. "Please, forgive my parents. I think they must have some sort of genetic defect that forces them to embarrass me every chance they get."

Her younger brother, Malachi, stood off to the side grinning from ear to ear.

She turned narrowed eyes on him and pointed a finger. "Not one word."

Malachi put his hands up, then with his right hand imitated a zipper closing over his mouth.

Cody couldn't help the chuckle. "It must be nice having a large family. I just have my grandpops, and while he can be a handful he also knows when to give me space." He pointed to the old man, who was watching from a distance.

Joseph Makinaw smiled and waved, then turned and headed toward the ol' coots' table, where he spent the rest of the night with his cronies, enjoying the good food and conversation.

"Can we trade families?" Sadie sighed and sat down at a round table.

"I suppose we could always find two chairs at a different table." Cody grinned and waggled his eyebrows.

"Thanks, but something tells me if we did that, my parents would ask the others at that table to move so we could all eat together." Sadie did not need to make any more scenes.

"True. Okay, how about we sit with your family, and any time you think they're going to say or do something embarrassing, you start to talk about the Christmas tree farm? That will be my cue to jump in with a tall tale."

Sadie couldn't help herself; she was liking this quiet cowboy more and more every day. Cody was the epitome of a gentleman, which was exactly what she needed.

And true to form, her parents couldn't help themselves.

The moment her mother sat down with her plate of food, she started in. "Sweetie, I don't want you to overtax yourself tonight, so no getting up and walking around. If you need anything, you let me or your father know." Then she proceeded to cut up Sadie's turkey and ham as though she was a little girl who couldn't be trusted to handle a knife.

Cody tried to hide his chuckle.

Sadie glared daggers at him, then turned to her mom. "Mother, it's my leg that's banged up, not my hands. I can cut my own food."

"Oh sweetie, I'm just trying to help, that's all." Mrs. McKinley took a tiny piece of turkey and dipped it in the gravy before trying to feed her daughter by hand.

Sadie pulled back. "I really miss the Christmas tree farm." She turned her head toward Cody, waiting for him to jump in and save her.

Cody got the message loud and clear. "Mrs. McKinley, did Sadie tell you about the trees she picked out for you and your family?"

Silvia's eyes perked up and she put the fork down on Sadie's plate. Sadie took the opportunity afforded by Cody's distraction and pulled the plate to her, along with her silverware.

"Really? How many trees? And how tall? Do tell." Silvia gave her full attention to Cody and ignored her daughter.

Sadie sat there eating the food on her plate all by herself, skipping the broccoli casserole. Her mother should never have put that on her plate. Sadie had always hated broccoli. Now, if she would have put the green bean casserole on her plate, that she would have eaten.

Sadie listened half-heartedly just so she would know when she needed to protect her food from her mother's interference when Cody's story was done. As she listened, she realized that when Cody had said "tall tale," he was being literal.

"I think Sadie picked out three of the fifteen-foot trees for y'all. I hope you have really high ceilings. I think you'll need at least a twenty-foot clearance for them, depending on how big your tree stand is and how tall your topper is." He winked at Sadie and kept talking about the trees, totally embellishing on how they looked, how thick the stems were, and anything else he could do to keep Mrs. McKinley distracted while Sadie ate.

Silvia's face went from excited to worried. Her eyes went between Cody and Sadie and she tried a couple of times to interrupt, but Cody kept going.

Sadie knew why her mom was so worried. If she wasn't so busy shoveling food into her face, she would have laughed. While they did have tall ceilings, only one of the giant trees would fit in the family room where they had a gorgeous view of the mountains. The highest spot in the formal living room would only allow for a ten-foot tree. And the entryway, where one of the trees was going to go, only had enough room for a standard seven- to eight-footer. She was enjoying this. If only it could have lasted.

A newcomer walked up to the table, and when Sadie looked up she just about choked over the turkey stuck in her throat.

"Sadie! Thank goodness. I thought you were in the hospital, dying." The unwanted man came quickly around the table and pulled her up into his arms in one fluid motion.

Cody was a bit slow on the uptake, so he wasn't out of his seat until the man was holding her tightly to his chest.

When Sadie finally got over the shock of seeing the six-foot-tall man with brown hair and a business suit, she was already in his arms.

The people all around them whispered and pointed, which only caused Sadie to freeze up. She hated public displays. And having all eyes on her at that moment only made her veins go cold. With food still in her mouth, she worked hard to swallow her ruined turkey dinner.

Cody looked from the man to Sadie and noticed her wide eyes. She looked back at him, hoping he would be able to understand. She sent a pleading gaze his way.

"Uh, who is this?" The entire room had gone quiet, and Cody only whispered it, but his question seemed to reverberate around the room.

The man holding Sadie pulled back only far enough to look Cody up and down. Then he put his arm around her waist. "I'm Wesley Watership, Sadie's fiancé."

The room was no longer quiet. Pandemonium broke out all over the place and people tried to get close. Some took out their phones and snapped pictures, and others turned their camera phones on video.

Sadie closed her eyes and hunched over. Then she realized what he had said and she stood up tall and turned an angry look on Wesley. "I am *not* your fiancé."

"Baby, of course you are. We talked about this." Wesley looked around the room and then leaned close to her ear. "Not here. We can discuss this back at your house."

Sadie pushed out of his hold and looked to Cody, who already had his back to her and was being swallowed up by the crowd wanting to get closer to hear everything being said. "Cody, wait."

Either he couldn't hear her or he didn't want to wait, but Cody Makinaw was out of there faster than she could break away from the table and all the well-wishers.

Chapter 20

"I knew it!" Cody pounded the wheel of the truck he was driving until he got his back from the shop. The moment he looked into Sadie's eyes, he knew that was the guy she'd left behind in Seattle. Only she'd told him a different story.

According what Sadie had said, that guy—Wesley Watership? It wouldn't surprise him if the suit was a third—was probably one of those yacht-club members who looked down on cowboys like Cody. What a name.

He had really broken up with her after she'd lost her job at a big advertising firm?

She'd never once said they were engaged. And to make matters worse, it sounded as though they had gotten back together.

Or had they never truly broken up?

Was this one of those Rachel and Ross breaks? Wesley, the punk, only wanted some time. Or was it she who wanted a little bit of time? And of course, he was the fool who'd started falling for the girl who wasn't truly available.

All this time they'd been talking and texting, you'd think she would have told him she was back with her ex. Cody had taken her out on an actual date. He deserved the truth.

Part of him wanted to turn around and head back to the dinner and find out what the jingle bells was going on with Sadie. But the realistic side told him to forget the girl. She wasn't worth his time or attention.

That Wesley Watership, yacht-club enthusiast, could have her.

When was he going to learn that women were more hassle, and heartache, than he needed? Sadie wasn't the first woman to lie to him.

When his phone began ringing, he figured it was Sadie calling him to come back. Which he wasn't ever going to do, so he ignored the calls until he arrived home.

Then it dawned on him, and he slapped his head. "Grandpops!" Cody pulled his phone out and looked at the messages. He had missed three calls and four text messages from his grandfather.

What a dingleberry he had been. And so selfish, too. Cody dialed his grandpops' phone and when the old man answered it, Cody apologized profusely and told him he was on his way back into town.

"Now hold up, son. Didn't you listen to my voicemail?" Grandpops asked.

"Uh"—Cody scratched his head and stopped the truck—"no, I just realized what I'd done and began to head back to get you."

"Daniel is bringing me home. Then you and I need to talk."

"About what?"

"About what?" Grandpops scoffed into his cell phone. "About leaving your date at the mercy of some crazy city boy."

"Grandpops, that's her fiancé."

"How do you know? Never mind, we'll talk when I get home. Put on the coffee." Grandpops hung up.

Cody hung his head in the cab of the borrowed truck and prayed for strength. He was going to need it to get through whatever his grandpops was about to say to him.

Cody had been sitting in the kitchen with a fresh cup of coffee in his hands when he heard the front door slam. Grandpops never slammed the door, except when he was hoppin' mad.

From experience, Cody knew he needed to sit tall and be confident. If he acted like a little boy, then his grandfather would treat him like one.

"Cody!" Grandpops bellowed the moment he entered the kitchen. "You fool. Sadie hobbled away on her crutches crying. That city slicker was close on her tail until her brother stopped him."

The truth of it stopped Cody's heart. He had abandoned the woman he was beginning to care for to some stranger who'd *claimed* to be her fiancé. Why hadn't he confirmed with Sadie before running off like a child who hadn't gotten their way?

All outer appearance of calm and indifference fled. Ice ran through his veins and he put his face in his hand. "What have I done?"

"You've done gone and lost the one woman who could have been your true partner in life. That woman"—Grandpops pointed in the general direction of where Sadie lived—"has done nothing but support you and help you. And all without any pay."

"I know, I know. It's because of her we're going to get at least another year in this place." Cody took a deep sigh and closed his eyes as they began to burn. He was a fool, and he knew it.

Silence filled the room, except for the sounds of Cody taking deep, shaky breaths.

Grandpops' shoulders relaxed and he grumbled something Cody couldn't understand. Then he went and poured himself a coffee. "Tomorrow is Sunday. You need to head into town early to see her." The old man turned around, and his eyes pinned Cody to his seat. "You better have the best apology known to man for that beautiful woman." He turned back around and said over his shoulder, "You don't deserve her."

Cody felt as though he was nothing better than a rat king. He had been raised to take better care of a woman. He never should have left her there. True, her family had been there with her, but she was his responsibility. His date. "I know, Grandpops. Trust me, I know."

Joseph sat at the table and took a drink of his coffee before getting down to the most important reason he wanted a heart-to-heart with his grandson. "Cody, we need to talk about the farm."

Cody knew it was time to have this discussion, but he really didn't have the energy to talk about it. "I know, and I'm doing everything I can to save the place. I'll not go down without a fight."

After a deep sigh, Cody's grandpops shook his head. "No, son. That's not what I meant."

"What did you mean?" Cody frowned and took a sip of his coffee. It was down to the last of his cup and he got up to get more.

His grandpops waited until he sat down. "Why are you working so hard to save the farm?"

Cody blinked and opened his mouth, "because it's our family farm. I'll not be the Makinaw so lets it go. This is my inheritance and I'm not screwing it up." He sighed. "Well, not any more than I already have. I think we're gonna save it."

"But do you really want this? I mean really and truly want to spend the rest of your life working the land and selling Christmas trees?"

Cody nodded. "Of course I do."

"Or do you just want to provide a place for me to live?"

"No," Cody shook his head. "I mean, yes I want to provide for you. But it's much more than that. I want to work hard here and provide a good life for me and my future family. And I want my kids to take over one day and not have to worry about money."

"So, you see yourself here on the land until you die?" Joseph narrowed his eyes and waited for his grandson to answer.

Cody scoffed. "Of course, I do. This place, this land, it's in my blood. Just like it's in your blood and was in my parents' blood. This is our family home, not just a tree farm."

Joseph tilted his head. "Are you sure? Would giving up the farm feel like giving up on your parents?"

While he did feel closer to his parents her on the farm more than any other place he'd ever been too, Cody didn't think he'd lose the memories of them if he left. "No, if I were to leave, it wouldn't be because I gave up on them. They will be with me wherever I go."

"And you know that your father and mother would be proud of you no matter what you did, right?" Joseph took another sip of his hot coffee.

Cody sighed. "I know they'd be disappointed if I lost the farm, but that isn't what drives me." He tilted his head. "Well, not all that drives me. Growing up here was the best. I want this for my future kids, if I ever have any."

Joseph chuckled. "Yes, this is the best place for kids to grow up. And you're still young. Don't worry, when the time is right, God will give you the family you want."

"I don't know about that."

Joseph rubbed his chin. "Are you still blaming God for taking your parents so young?"

Cody sat there thinking about what his grandpops had asked and slowly shook his head. "No, I don't think so." He didn't want to go into it any more than that. At that moment, Cody really wasn't sure how to explain the changes he'd been going through the past weeks. Sadie had been great, but God had been better. The time he had spent reading the Bible and praying was changing his heart.

"Good, good. Because you know that we all have a designated time here on Earth. Nothing we do will change that timeline for us."

"I know, grandpops. Listen, I'm really tired and just want this day to be over with." Cody stood and took his cup to the sink to rinse out.

"Fine, fine." Joseph waved his hand. "But, you need to talk to that woman. She's the one God has chosen for you, and I know it, here." He pointed to his heart.

Not wanting to hear any more about how he'd screwed up, Cody went to his room to pray. There was a verse in the back of his mind about giving everything to God. He needed to put his burdens at the feet of God and ask for mercy in addition to forgiveness. Not that he deserved it.

He spent the next hour praying that God would give him the words to say to Sadie, and also that He would take care of her. With the two brothers being so protective of her, Sadie should be physically safe. But he wanted the woman to be emotionally safe as well.

It was time he cowboyed up and did the right thing.

Chapter 21

S adie couldn't believe her eyes. The man she had come to count on, the one she wanted to spend her time with and give her heart to, had up and abandoned her. Just like Wesley had done all those months ago.

Now, the frustrating man was back. It wasn't easy, but she hobbled around and glared at Wesley. They needed to talk, but not here. Knowing he would make a scene if she said a thing to him, she headed outside to see if she could catch a ride with anyone who'd take her home. Since she knew most people in this area, Sadie wasn't worried about any trouble from one of her neighbors.

"Sadie, wait," Wesley called after her.

When she made her way outside and found someone to take her home, she thought about what she had just done. In a sense, she'd pulled a Cody. Although, Wesley deserved to be left behind. She did not.

Who did Wesley think he was to come to her hometown on the night of the community Thanksgiving dinner and make a scene in front of all her family and friends? How dare he announce to the town that they were engaged? Rage filled her as she thought of the look on Cody's face.

Then she deflated and realized what Cody must have thought.

Sadie wanted to deny Wesley's statement. They weren't engaged. But they had talked about it before she was let go from her job. They were making plans. At least until he decided she wasn't good enough for him anymore.

Now, eight months later, after not a single word from him, he'd shown up during Frenchtown's busiest night of the year and embarrassed her in front of not only Cody, but her family? The dingleberry deserved a slap on the face for what he'd done.

"Thanks, George. Have a good night." She closed the door of her neighbor's truck and ignored any offer of help from him or his wife. All she wanted to do now was get inside and make a cup of peppermint tea. Then sit in her room and pray for God to help her through this.

"What a mess." Sadie went about putting the tea kettle on and getting her favorite coffee mug. Well, her old favorite mug; it had the logo of the tree farm on it. One of the many items she had helped Cody create for the season. Now, she wanted to bash it against the wall.

Instead, she pulled out a regular Christmas coffee mug and put her tea bag and sugar in it while she waited for the kettle to whistle.

A watched pot never boils is so true. After what felt like forever, but was most likely only a handful of minutes, the steam exited the tiny hole at the end of the spout, followed by a high-pitched whistle. The sort that always gave Sadie a headache. But tonight, she already had one thanks to a stupid cowboy.

By the time she was in her comfy pajamas and sipping her hot tea, she heard the truck pull up outside. She knew it was her parents because of the backfire that sounded when the engine turned off. A tiny voice in the back of her mind had hoped it would be Cody coming to say he was sorry and that he'd made a giant mistake, then grovel at her feet for forgiveness.

It was a stupid wish, and she knew it. In her experience, men never groveled. They rarely even said they were sorry.

She had just gotten down on her knees to spend some quality time with God when she heard a light knock at her door.

"Sade?" Her little brother, Malachi, couldn't pronounce her name properly when he was just learning to speak. In fact, it had taken him years to pronounce her name correctly, and every now and then he reverted back to her childhood nickname.

She sighed and got up off her knees and sat in her chair. "Come in, Malachi."

She expected to see a blond head come around the door. Instead, when she saw pink skin with black spots and a pirate patch over one eye, she couldn't help but smile. "Pirate Spot. Come on in."

Malachi had held his pet pig through the doorway for Sadie to see first, knowing it would be the only thing to make her smile. Then his blond hair entered before the rest of his scraggly body. Even though Malachi was twenty-two and built well, he had always been the runt of the litter in the McKinley family. He was the shortest at just five feet, six inches tall.

"Hey, sis. How ya holdin' up?" Her brother and his pig came closer to her. Malachi picked up the pig and put it on her bed when he sat down.

Sadie blew out a deep sigh. "Not so good."

"I'm sorry, but I've gotta know. Are you really engaged to that wanker?" Malachi pointed over his shoulder toward the town center, where he had left a confused Wesley standing there right after Sadie left.

She shook her head. "Not that I've ever been aware of. But you know men, they think what they want."

Malachi tilted his head. "Why would he say that?"

"To get rid of Cody…and make a scene." Sadie had actually wondered the same thing. And all she could come up with was that Wes had noticed how she and Cody were sitting close to each other and had gotten jealous.

"Are you going to call Cody?" Malachi flinched when his sister's eyes shot daggers at him.

"Of course not." She wanted to go on, but her brother didn't really want to hear what she thought about Cody leaving her there.

"And what about Wesley?"

Feeling exhausted, she slumped down even farther in her chair and shook her head. "I don't know. I guess I'll call him tomorrow. He'd been trying to get ahold of me all day. Maybe there's something he really does need to tell me. I don't know." It finally dawned on her that if she had just picked up one of his many calls or texts, she could have avoided the scene tonight.

But since they hadn't spoken in almost a year, she didn't really want to know what he had to say. And she was too busy thinking about Cody and the community Thanksgiving dinner.

This event was huge for Frenchtown. Every year since the town was first incorporated, they got together to share a meal and give thanks for the bounty they had received that year. Even when times were tough, they always got together to give thanks.

Sadie was sure she was being overly dramatic, but it felt as though Wesley and Cody had both ruined the night for the entire town, but most especially for her.

The next morning she woke with a headache and lay there wishing she was already past this day. Even though she loved Sundays and going to church, she just wanted to fast forward and skip all of the awkward moments and questions that were sure to come her way.

Instead, she got up and got ready, then went downstairs for a large mug of coffee before heading to Sunday services. Even though she wasn't going to the tree farm or lot today, Sadie still enjoyed the early service. It had nothing to do with the fact that most of her family and friends would be at the regular services today instead of the early one. Nope, she wasn't avoiding anyone or anything.

She continued to tell herself that as she left her house, and didn't realize she had been scanning the front yard and the street in front of her place for signs of either man.

The music for church that day was soothing and just what she needed to get in the spirit for a message from God. But when the pastor started his lesson, Sadie rolled her eyes, then looked up and silently asked, *Really, God? This is the message you wanted me to get today?*

It wasn't that it was a bad message, or even off-track. In fact, it was spot-on for her situation. The only problem was that she wasn't ready to hear it. As she sat there following along in her Bible and really paying attention to the words coming out of the pastor's mouth, she realized her prayers hadn't gone unanswered like she thought.

No, God was telling her, again, what he'd told her last night. She needed to forgive. While she got that part of the message, what she didn't get was *who* it was she needed to forgive.

Did God want her to forgive Wesley and maybe even get back with him? For that did seem to be what he'd wanted last night when he told everyone they were engaged. Even though he had never actually proposed. They had only started talking about the possibility while they were still dating. Before she came home, it was what she had wanted, wasn't it?

Sadie even remembered praying that Wesley would hurry up and propose so they could get on with their lives. When it never happened and he broke her heart, Sadie had wished they'd been engaged before she lost her job. Surely he wouldn't have broken off the engagement just because she didn't have a job. Would he?

God spoke to her as she thought these things and He said a resounding, *Of course he would have.* Which only served to help her understand that even when it seemed God wasn't answering her prayers, He really was. It just wasn't the answer she wanted to hear.

Now she wondered if she needed to forgive Cody for abandoning her the previous night.

While Cody didn't deserve her forgiveness, she was commanded to forgive him.

The Pastor read a verse out of Matthew that really hit her hard:

"'For if ye forgive men their trespasses, your heavenly Father will also forgive you. But if ye forgive not men their trespasses, neither will your Father forgive your trespasses. Matthew 6:14-15.'"

All thoughts of who she should forgive, or who she should ignore, left her head. The Lord had given her His answer in those two short verses.

Sadie had to forgive both Wesley and Cody. It didn't matter if they deserved it—God commanded it. Who was she—someone who'd sinned so many times in her past, and even recently—to receive forgiveness from God? If she didn't do what God was telling her, He wouldn't forgive her.

And since God treated all equally, her little white lies that she told on very rare occasions, or her naughty thoughts that sometimes crept up on her when she was watching things she knew God didn't like, wouldn't be forgiven.

Of course, that didn't mean she would lose her salvation. It only meant that God would punish her later for what she had done, and what she most likely will do again in the future. One thing Sadie had learned in her thirty-two years was that she still made mistakes.

No one was perfect. But God still forgave His children.

How could she in all good conscience not offer forgiveness to the two men who had hurt her? She would forgive them. It didn't mean she had to get back together with Wesley, or even continue to date Cody. It just meant she could no longer hold onto the anger and frustration, or even heartache, that they had caused her.

She imagined what all of mankind's sins had done to God over the centuries and millennia. And He said He would forgive man. She could do no less.

When the service was over, she looked around the room to see if Wesley had shown up, or even Cody. While she preferred to speak with Wesley first, she saw Cody there, looking at her with sad, puppy-dog eyes.

Even though Sadie wasn't Catholic, she had an urge to cross herself. It was silly, really, but she needed something comforting at that moment to give her the strength to do what she knew was needed.

And as that thought crossed her mind, God spoke to her heart: *I am here*.

Energy flowed through her veins, and she had the confidence she needed to do this. In the background, a CD played "Our God is an Awesome God." And she knew He truly was.

"Good morning, Cody." Inwardly, Sadie shook like a tree during a blustery day. But outwardly, she was calm, cool, and collected.

"Sadie." Cody sighed, then winced. "I'm so sorry for leaving you last night. I know that was stupid and immature." He glanced to his left; people were stopping and looking at them. "Maybe we can go somewhere private and talk?"

Sadie looked around, then rolled her eyes at the gossipmongers who were just waiting for something juicy to share all over town. "Of course."

Chapter 22

They walked outside to a light snowfall of soft flakes, the sort that would land and leave a downy, soft layer of fresh snow. Cody helped Sadie put her coat on before he put his on. Then he pulled the hood of her coat up over her head.

Once they were both dressed for the weather, he guided her to his borrowed truck. What he wanted was to take her to the park and sit on a bench. But with the temperature dropping, he knew they wouldn't be able to sit outside for long. If all went well, he'd take her for some hot coffee at Lottie's store.

"Cody, I forgive you." She chuckled and looked down at her hands fidgeting in her lap. "How could I not after a sermon like that?"

Cody winced and realized she hadn't wanted to forgive him. At least, not yet. But he couldn't let it end like this. "Does this mean you're gonna get back with your ex?" He knew Sadie and Wesley weren't truly together, but that didn't mean she didn't want to get back with him. Sadie had told him that she was with her ex for a long time. People didn't just walk away from serious relationships that easily.

He should know.

But as he also had learned in his past, sometimes it was best to walk away with your head held high. What he and Sadie had was only just beginning. While he did want to see where this led, he also knew that they weren't committed to one another, and she didn't owe him anything.

It was a few moments before Sadie said anything, and in that time, Cody's heart stopped. He realized he'd read the situation all wrong and she was going to get back with him. Was it his fault? Did he shove her into the other man's arms when he didn't stand up to the guy and make his own intentions known? Sure, he wasn't ready to ask for her hand in marriage—it was way too soon for that. But, he could have said something, anything to let Sadie know he was hers.

"I… I'm not sure. I need to speak with Wes." She looked up at him. "And just so you know, we were never engaged. We spoke about it, but he was taking his own sweet time with the proposal." Sadie sighed. "So, I'm not really sure what's going on right now."

Cody nodded. "I understand."

She shook her head. "Do you? Because I don't. All I know is that I gave Wes my heart a long time ago. He threw it back at me when I lost my job. But now? I don't know."

His head was telling him that she wasn't totally gone. Not yet. But his heart? Well, that was a different story. It was breaking as though she had frozen it and then shot a bullet straight through.

However, could he just sit there and do nothing? Could he let her walk away from their budding relationship? Not without saying one thing first.

Cody looked at Sadie's bowed head, and using his forefinger, he lifted her head by the chin. "Sadie, I never would have broken up with you just because you lost a job. I don't know what your relationship was like with that…that…cad. But a real man takes care of his woman when she needs help."

She interrupted, "Then why did you walk away last night?"

He opened his mouth to say something and then lowered his head. "I'm so sorry. That was stupid of me, and I'll always regret it. At that moment, I thought he was telling the truth. Especially when you didn't deny it."

"You didn't give me time to say anything. You ran off like a scared little rabbit. I thought real cowboys stood by their woman and weren't afraid of anything."

His head popped up. "No, we are afraid. But you're right about one thing, a real cowboy wouldn't run away like I did. The moment I was on the road, I realized what I had done was wrong. There's no excuse, but the situation reminded me of someone else. Someone else who had gone and got herself engaged while I was burying my parents."

Sadie gasped. "I had no idea, Cody." She put a hand on his shoulder. "What happened?"

Cody turned his head to look out his window, covering his mouth with his hand. "Does it really matter? That was a long time ago." He turned to look at her and sadness filled his entire being. "I thought you and I were starting something real. But I understand if you want to go back to your old boyfriend and leave Frenchtown." Not wanting to look at her beautiful face anymore, Cody turned to look straight ahead and put his hands on his steering wheel. "It's getting cold—you should probably get inside. And I have the tree farm to open."

Out of the corner of his eye, he witnessed Sadie bite her lower lip and wipe a tear away from her cheek. "I'm sorry I hurt you. I truly do wish you and your farm all the success in the world."

"Thank you." Cody knew he would never be where he was if it weren't for Sadie's help. "I couldn't have done this without you. Maybe your time here was a gift from God and it was never meant to be more than that."

She nodded. "Merry Christmas, Cody."

"Merry Christmas, Sadie."

He watched while she walked away, not looking back. Then it was his turn to wipe a tear from his cheek.

Unbeknownst to them both, Mr. and Mrs. Claus were parked right next to them and had witnessed their conversation. Even though the windows were rolled up, Mrs. Claus had keen hearing and had overheard most of what they'd said.

"Chris, I really thought that calendar idea would have gotten them together." Jessica Lambton, AKA Mrs. Claus, watched Sadie walk away and prayed that she'd turn back and look at Cody.

Christopher Lambton, AKA Santa Claus, shook his head. "You can bring a horse to water, but you can't make it drink."

Jessica pursed her lips. "I declare, sometimes men can be so heartless." She crossed her arms.

Chris grinned. "Oh, come now, sweetheart. You know it's true. Those two are as stubborn as mules. It's just going to take a little extra work on your part."

"And yours." She pointed her index finger and her husband while trying to hide a smile.

Chapter 23

L ater that evening, Sadie found herself wishing she hadn't invited Wesley over to talk. They were both sitting in her family's living room, with her mother acting as a chaperone, and Wesley didn't seem likely to leave any time soon.

Sadie's mother seemed confused. One minute Silvia was smiling at Wesley, and the next she was frowning behind his back. It appeared her mother had the same feelings as she did— unsure what to make of this man.

"Wesley, while I thank you for the latest gossip from Seattle, I think it's time you told my why you're here." Sadie rubbed at her right temple, feeling a headache coming on. It was nice to hear how some of their friends where faring. Although, none of them seemed to care about her once she left town.

Her so-called "friends" hadn't been very communicative over the past months. In the beginning they were good about taking her calls and emailing her back. But since summer, they had for the most part been quiet. Sadie noticed that not one of them ever reached out to her first. In fact, they rarely even picked up her calls. And not one message had been returned for the past few months.

It seemed the people she had called friends for years really weren't her friends after all. Or maybe it was just how it went when someone moved to a different state? Didn't she lose touch with her high school friends not too long after moving to Seattle?

When Wesley opened his mouth to speak, she turned her full attention on him. "Sadie, darling, I missed you. Why haven't you picked up any of my calls or returned my texts?"

Full of indignation, for Wes had only begun calling and texting Saturday morning, she crossed her arms and pursed her lips. "Where were you when I lost my job?"

A cloud passed over Wesley's eyes before he turned his charm back on. "Dear heart, I was working hard to get you hired back."

A bold-faced lie, and she knew it. If he had been trying to get her hired back, he would have at least stayed in touch with her. Instead, the moment he broke up with her he became a ghost. It was almost as though he had blocked all of her ways to contact him. Either that, or he'd just ignored her.

Sadie had tried to reach out to him several times after he broke up with her, but when Wes ignored her pleas for help, she left the city and went home. He could have helped her get a new job if he had really cared for her.

"Darling, I have a new job for you. I'm so sorry it's taken so long, but I figured you coming home to see your family would be good for you. It gave me time to network on your behalf and find the perfect company for you." He sat back, pride evident in the way his shoulders straightened, and he held his head high.

What this new job was all about confused Sadie, but a memory surfaced of a social media post she saw before leaving town and unfriending the lout. "Let me guess, you've been wining and dining all the single, beautiful hiring managers in town?"

He blinked. "What do you mean?"

"I mean I saw pictures of you taking various women out to dinner. In fact, one of them was taken the day after you broke things off with me." It had hurt to see him smiling and obviously happy, especially since Sadie was still crying her eyes out. Not only because he broke up with her, but because she seemed to be blackballed in the city. Not a single hiring manager would return her calls or emails.

Someone had spread the word that she wasn't to be hired. While Sadie doubted it was Wesley—he wasn't that mean and vindictive—she knew he wasn't trying at all to get her a job. No, that woman in the photo Sadie had seen had nothing to do with hiring or HR. She was one of the sales managers at Wesley's company.

"Sweetheart, I was only meeting with people I thought could help you get your career back on track. That's all." He put a hand out to touch her, and Sadie scooted away.

"Wes, tell me." Sadie narrowed her eyes as she thought about the name of the woman in that picture. "How is Vanessa doing these days?"

First shock, then something else crossed Wesley's face, and she knew she had his number.

"Why are you really here?"

Wesley cleared his throat and sat back in his chair. "I was telling the truth. I'm here for you, and I have a job offer from one of the best marketing firms in the city."

His words rang true about the job, but she also knew there was more to it. Wes may have an offer for her, but he wouldn't have come all this way and offered marriage if there wasn't something big in it for him. But she'd play his game, only long enough to discover what he was hiding. "And what is the job offer?"

Excitement now covered Wes's face. He must have thought he had her. When he sat forward, he licked his lips. "One of the premier marketing agencies in the country contacted me and wants to hire you as their newest marketing manager. They have clients who want you to design their new marketing campaigns. In fact, I was hoping to bring you back with me tomorrow so you can start right away."

When he named the company and their salary package, she almost jumped up and said, "Let's go now." But a small voice in the back of her head told her this was too good to be true. As that old adage came to the forefront of her mind, she knew there was something else going on here, and she needed to get to the bottom of it.

It only took Sadie a few moments to get herself under control and take on the visage of someone who was excited and happy to be going back to Seattle in such style. "Really? That's wonderful. How did you get this for me?"

A sly grin appeared on Wesley's face for a moment, and Sadie knew she had the right of it. "I was having lunch with one of the partners in the agency. My company also does work with them, and he asked me about you. He remembered that you and I dated."

"Really?" Sadie arched a brow, wondering how Wes would have covered up the fact that he had dumped her when she needed him the most.

He nodded. "I told him you'd gone home to prepare for our upcoming wedding."

A lot of information must have passed between Wesley and the executive to make him say he was marrying her. "What did he say about that?"

"Why, of course he congratulated me and asked when the big wedding was."

A desire to cross her arms over her chest and smirk came and went. Instead, she smiled and looked at him longingly. "And when are we getting married, my love?"

When his head shot back, she thought she must have overdone it. Then a satisfied grin covered his face. He moved closer and took her hand. "I thought we'd get married in the spring, when everything is in bloom. Since you've been here this whole time, I figured we'd be having the ceremony here."

"Of course, and that would make it more difficult for anyone in Seattle to expect an invitation, which would explain why no one had even received an announcement yet, correct?"

She knew she had him on the ropes when he nodded.

"You understand," he asked, "don't you?"

Oh, she understood alright. He needed her to get back to town and take this job for some strange reason, and once it was all finalized, he'd find some way to break up with her, again. Sadie wondered how long she'd have to play his game before he showed his cards.

"Of course, my darling." She squeezed his hand. "Where's my ring?"

When he looked confused, she wondered if he had even thought that far.

"Engagement ring, dear. I can't go back to the city without one. Especially if we're already making so many plans for the wonderful wedding. No one will believe you really want to marry me if I don't have a ring." Oh, was it difficult to keep from laughing. Sadie tried so hard. But when Wesley started turning white, she had to turn her head and cough to cover up the smile about to explode from her.

If only they had a security camera inside the house. She'd love to watch this later, after she found out what was happening. She so desperately wanted to laugh and enjoy the discomfort that Wesley had to be feeling.

"Oh, right." He cleared his throat. "I didn't bring it with me. I was in such a hurry to get here that I must have left it back at my apartment." He nodded and mumbled something she couldn't understand. "When we get home, I'll plan a nice dinner and propose properly."

As though she were acting out a scene in a fluffy romance movie, Sadie tilted her head and clapped her hands over her chest. "My darling, you really have thought of everything, haven't you?"

Wesley breathed a sigh of relief, and he took her hand again. "Yes, my dear, I believe I have."

"And what will my job be? You said they already have clients they want me to work with? I assume they'll be alright with me bringing my current clientele with me as well." The current clients Sadie had weren't the reason this company was after her. They couldn't be. None of them would bring in millions; they were all small companies. Well, one had the ability to grow into a large company down the road. But unless one of her clients was about to be acquired, she doubted the partners at Blue Sky Marketing had even thought of obtaining their business.

Wesley nodded. "Of course, you can bring whomever you want along." He gave her a condescending pat on the hand. "But you'll want to make sure the majority of your time is spent working on your new client's behalf."

"And who would that be?" She batted her lashes and appeared on the outside as though she didn't have a care in the world. But on the inside, she was bubbling with excitement. The new client must be someone big. Maybe one of her old clients at her former company? They might have said they'd leave if Blue Sky had her. She wracked her brain trying to think of her largest clients, but only one stood out as being large enough to get Blue Sky excited to bring her back to town.

Wesley licked his lips and stretched the silence between them, probably thinking that being dramatic would get her all worked up, and then she'd be so grateful to him that she'd forget all about the fact that he didn't bring a ring.

Wesley pulled his hand back and rubbed them together. Then he leaned forward and whispered, "Elliot Plastics Manufacturing." He sat back with an expectant look on his face.

Sadie thought Wesley might be waiting for her to jump up and down with excitement. But she was confused. What did a plastics manufacturer want with her skills? She'd heard of them, of course, but theirs weren't the sort of products she'd worked with in the past. She wouldn't have been surprised if he'd named one of the larger banks or financial companies in the country. But a manufacturing brand wanting her? She didn't get it.

When she said nothing, the excitement on Wesley's face began to fade. "Aren't you excited? They're one of the largest manufacturers in the country. And they want you to manage their account."

"Yeah, I know who they are, but I don't get it. I've never worked with physical products before."

He interrupted, "But you have."

Slowly, she responded, "But not on a large scale. And that was straight out of college, when I was an intern."

Wesley shook his head. "Think about it. What have you been doing since you came home?"

After a mental recap of her current clients, she realized her only client that didn't have her managing marketing for services was the Big Sky Christmas tree farm. "What does Cody's family farm have to do with manufacturing?"

Again with the condescending look. Sadie began to wonder what she had seen in Wesley. Memories of how he had poo-pooed her worries, or downplayed her previous achievements, resurfaced. And then she wondered if he really did want her back for some real reason. She couldn't understand what she had that this manufacturing company might want.

Why would anyone care that she was helping a struggling tree farm get out of the red? If the farm made money, that wouldn't affect anyone else. Well, except for maybe the competing tree lots. But Cody had said he didn't have many that he supplied in other states.

The other lot in Frenchtown couldn't have anything to do with a manufacturing company, either. She scratched her head and wracked her brain, trying for the life of her to figure out what was going on.

The cocky Wesley that had always bugged her came out. "I take it you haven't been paying attention to the Seattle newspapers?"

She shook her head. "No, why should I? I moved home and was making my life here."

"Because if you had been paying attention, you would have noticed that Elliot Plastics has recently been buying up live Christmas tree farms." He paused and waited for her to catch on.

"Sooo, they want me to help them acquire Big Sky Christmas Tree Farm?" Sadie knew that if Cody didn't make enough this year, he'd have to sell out. Although, with everything they'd done so far, he was very close to not only saving his farm, but also having the seed money he'd need to expand their business.

Would a company as large as Elliot Plastics really care about one little tree farm that might or might not be able to start doing a local pumpkin patch and carnival?

"What they want is for you to turn things around for the artificial Christmas tree market. It seems your push to help this local tree farm has had a far-reaching impact on the artificial tree market."

Sadie couldn't help it—she let the grin she'd been holding back come forth. "You mean to say that Cody's tree farm is doing so well that it's cut profits from a major manufacturer of artificial Christmas trees?"

"No, not just his farm. It was the marketing campaign you and that old fart did about real trees actually being better for the environment and the plastic tree hurting the environment." A sour look crossed Wesley's face. "That little stunt you pulled with the old coot worked. Using an old man to get your posts trending was ingenious. Now there's outcries all over the country about the manufacturing process of artificial trees and how much it's hurting the ozone layer." He scoffed. "The tree huggers have all united."

"Uh, was that pun intended?" Sadie couldn't help making fun of him. Now she knew why he was working so hard. Elliot Plastics was one of his company's largest clients.

A frosty chill passed between the two of them, and she knew he had zero interest in her at all. His client had asked him to get her to stop what she was doing, and they would do anything they could to get her to use her marketing insights to turn the industry upside down, again. While Sadie did love a good fake tree, and there were plenty of places they were needed, she also preferred a real tree whenever possible. And she'd never want to hurt Cody, or the real tree market.

While Sadie recycled and did her part to save the Earth, she wasn't what one would call a tree hugger. Well, unless it was a real Christmas tree—then she might hug one. And she was reminded of an old t-shirt she had: *Save the Earth, it's the only planet with chocolate*. She'd do whatever it took to save chocolate. And promoting real, live trees did help.

As she had done her research, she'd discovered that growing Christmas trees helped save the planet, in a way—the trees produced more oxygen. Even though metric tons of trees were cut down every year, they were also replaced. So it was a renewable source of trees that didn't hurt the environment.

And she had nothing against manufacturing, either. A lot of things she enjoyed and couldn't live without, like her cell phone, computer, truck, and so many more, were created via manufacturing plants. Without the industrial revolution, they'd still be driving horse and buggies and never even know what a phone was. Or worse, the internet.

However, she did recognize the fact that manufacturing could sometimes cause more pollution than anything else. Even more than plastic straws. What they needed was another industrial revolution, one where the machinery used to make products stopped polluting the Earth. They needed more clean energy sources. But until it could be done, they couldn't stop manufacturing the items the world used daily. And that included Christmas trees.

These were the conflicting thoughts rolling around her head when she noticed Wesley trying to get her attention.

"Sorry, I was thinking about what you said. This is a lot to take in." While there wasn't some sort of conspiracy at play here, Wesley was trying to stop her from helping Cody. Which was exactly why he had said they were engaged.

Wesley had always been great at reading his opponents. He'd watch them and see what their weakness was, then go in for the kill.

She had been so stupid.

Of course, Wesley had pushed the right buttons to get Cody out of the picture, and have her doubt him. She would have bet a million dollars he had been in town for a few days getting the lay of the land and discovering exactly how to get Sadie to leave and stop helping the enemy. That, of course, was how Wesley would have seen Cody. Not because they were dating, but because Cody was the one who got Sadie to work with Joseph on the environmental aspects of choosing a real tree over a fake one.

Sadie took the time she needed in order to get her thoughts in line.

"How long before the manufacturing of Christmas trees begins to drop so low that your client loses too much money?" The root of all evil was money, and Sadie knew this all too well. That was part of why she had lost her job in the first place: she didn't want to support a company that put profits ahead of people.

"I knew you'd understand." Wesley relaxed and grinned the sort of grin that said he knew he'd won. "Our analysts predict in only five years' time, the industry will begin to crumble. Losses will outstrip profits."

"I see. And Blue Sky is aware of the situation?" Just because Elliot Plastics might be in trouble, it didn't necessarily mean that

Blue Sky Marketing was in on the plan to put tree farms out of business.

"To an extent, yes. Which is why they want you. If you can turn your campaign around, it will do a lot to alleviate the pressure the artificial tree market is starting to feel. It could even make a difference this year if you get started right away."

Sadie knew what she was going to do, but she wasn't sure how to do it without making an enemy of Wesley. In no way did she ever think her marketing campaign would have hurt another industry. But it made sense. If people began buying real trees again, they wouldn't be buying fake Christmas trees. Which meant that the manufacturers would lose money.

But on the other hand, she had never intended for an entire industry to be affected so dramatically, so fast. Sadie only wanted to help save the Big Sky Christmas Tree Farm, not the entire real-tree market.

Chapter 24

C ody had blown it with Sadie, and he knew it. It was now Monday and he truly thought that Sadie would have called by now, but she hadn't.

His only real friend in town was nowhere to be seen. Who would he talk to about Sadie and how to fix this? He really did want to keep going with Sadie. But would she want to go back to Seattle with that *guy*? He was such a dingleberry.

Again, Cody texted his friend and farm foreman, Daniel. And nothing came back. An hour later, after Cody was about to give up and go seek advice from his grandpops, he got a call from Daniel.

"It's about time. Where have you been?" Cody's voice was extra gruff, but he didn't care. It wasn't Daniel's day off and the cowboy had disappeared without a word to anyone.

"I'm so sorry, boss. Megan had a family emergency and she needed me to help her." Daniel's voice sounded strained.

"Is she alright?" Cody was trying to process this new information. He knew Daniel liked the counselor from the Crooked Arrow Ranch, but he didn't know that they had come to the point where she would call him for help.

"I'm not really sure, yet. I think she will be. But, well…here's the thing." The line went quiet before Cody heard Daniel's voice again. "I'm going to be gone for a few days."

"What? Why? Wait, are you already gone?" A sinking feeling entered the pit of Cody's stomach. He couldn't do this without his foreman, or best friend.

"I'm sorry, I really am." A long and heavy sigh could be heard over the line. "But she needs me. I can't leave her alone through this."

"What's going on?"

"I can't tell you. She'll have to be the one to say something when we return. Just know that I wouldn't have done this if it wasn't an emergency. Can you get Sadie to help?"

"Ah, that. I guess you haven't heard the latest." Cody sat down and gave Daniel the highlights. He knew something had gone wrong on Saturday night, but he must not have heard it all.

"Oh, man. I'm sorry. But"—Daniel paused—"don't you think you could at least patch things up enough to get her help? This whole season is because of her. I'm sure she'd want to help you if you went to her with an olive branch."

"I tried that. She wants nothing to do with me. I think she's going to take her ex back and leave." A sour taste entered Cody's mouth and his stomach began to hurt.

"No, I don't believe she's going to leave you or this town. I've seen the two of you together and I've noticed how she looks at you. She might be mad right now, but she's not going to leave with some yacht-club guy."

Cody could have laughed as Daniel described Wesley Watership the same exact way he had. "Women do the strangest things."

"True."

"Alright, Daniel. Let me know when you're coming home and if there's anything I can do to help you."

"Thanks, man. I appreciate it. Prayers are probably the only thing that can help now." Daniel hung up.

Cody wondered what his friend had gotten himself into if prayer was the only thing that could help at this point. And he worried about how he was going to manage everything without Sadie and Daniel, the two people he had relied on the most to get everything going this year.

Prayer? Could he do it? Would God still be there listening to him after Cody hadn't really been open to listening to what God had to say to him all these years? His prayer life and relationship with God had been changing over the past few weeks, but to rely solely on God? That was tough.

That night, after dinner and time talking to his grandpops about God, as well as too many other things, Cody knew what he had to do.

Once Cody was in his room, he got down on his knees and rested his elbows on his bed.

"God, I know you love me and have just been waiting for me to come back to you. I'm so sorry I strayed so far away. Your plan is always perfect. I may not understand why you let some things happen, but I have been listening lately. I know that evil has a firm grasp on this planet, and we are the ones responsible for letting the enemy take over. We've become complacent, and lazy. *I've* become complacent and lazy."

Cody understood it was the responsibility of mankind to stand up the pressures of society and the biggest enemy that man had, the devil. That didn't mean it was easy, though. Sitting back and letting small things slide was so much easier than standing up for what was right.

He'd seen it plenty of times on social media. Not that Cody was big on social media, but his grandpops was. And his grandpops loved to share. Herd mentality was difficult to stand up to. Sin was always so much prettier, and easier, than doing what was right.

"Please forgive me for blaming you for my parents' death and everything that's happened ever since. I know we all have an appointed time for death. One day, when I'm in heaven with you, I'll understand why you took my parents when you did. Until then, I'm choosing to trust your decision. And I'm apologizing for railing against you for everything. It's not your fault that sin entered this world, it's our own. I have the ability to stand up and say no, but I chose to sit back and sulk instead of move forward."

His mind was going all over the place, thinking about all of his bad decisions, as well as what he *should* have done differently. While he couldn't change what he had done, or thought, in the past, he could do better going forward.

"Thank you, Lord for forgiving my doubt, and for welcoming me back into your open arms."

All of the messages Cody had heard lately seemed to be directed at him, and his need to repent. Even thought it wouldn't be easy, he was going to get back into attending church regularly and even start up a daily devotional time.

He'd seen his grandpops studying the Bible in the mornings. Maybe Cody could ask him where to start.

The next day when he went into his office early to look at the books, he realized that they were going to need another printing of the calendar before the end of the week. Picking up the phone, he also realized he didn't know the number to the printer. That was something Sadie had always taken care of.

Getting help to feed the animals and make sure the grounds were ready for the lot to open wasn't difficult, but the business side—or Sadie's side—was going to be almost impossible. He needed to see her one more time and get all of her information and plans for the season before she left town.

In Cody's mind, it wasn't a matter of *if*, but *when*. He had already resigned himself to her leaving, and most likely soon. When he put the phone down, he began praying and asking God for guidance on what to do next. Cody knew he couldn't do this without help. And with his two best helpers gone—one temporarily absent while the other one would be permanent—he knew where to go for help.

Even with straw on the ground, it was tough on one's knees. However, Cody reasoned that getting down on his knees was much easier than dying on the cross. So he prayed. Not only for his needs, but Megan's. While Cody didn't know what was going on, God did. And he also prayed for Sadie. While he didn't want the pretty cowgirl to leave, he knew it wasn't up to him. If God wanted her back in Seattle, then that was where she needed to be.

So when a feminine voice interrupted his prayers, he had to blink a few times to convince himself she was really standing there.

"Sadie?"

"Cody, I'm so sorry, I didn't mean to interrupt your prayers." She started to back away.

He stood up. "Don't worry, I was actually finishing up when I heard you. It's funny how God's timing is always perfect."

"You have no idea." She practically snorted, then covered her mouth.

For the first time in days, Cody grinned.

"Uh, can we talk?" When a woman said that, men usually ran for cover. It almost always meant the guy was in trouble. But since he knew he had already been in trouble, and he'd done nothing after he apologized, his mind went blank. He was clueless as to what she might want.

"Sure. Have a seat." Cody motioned to one of the chairs that didn't have calendars stacked on it. These were the last ones he had, other than what was already up at the registers for the tree farm and lot. And those wouldn't last long.

Sweat began to form on Cody's brow. It wasn't the least bit hot in the office. It was in fact, a bit chilly. The cowboy worried about what might come out of Sadie's mouth. He prayed she wasn't here to tell him that she was marrying the son of a nutcracker who came to town to steal her away.

"I spoke to Wesley Sunday night." Sadie lowered her gaze and picked at her fingers.

This was it, she was going to tell him she was now engaged. A feeling of unease stuck in his stomach and he wished he could drink an entire bottle of the pink stuff and it would take away the sickness beginning to take over.

Cody felt his old ways returning, and the Grinch was about to make a return. But he held himself in check and his face was devoid of all emotion as he waited to hear what she had to say.

Her nostrils flared, and she gulped before telling him all about Wesley and how he tried to trick her into returning with him so she could be used to put Cody's tree farm out of business.

"What? I mean…" Cody scratched his chin. He hadn't shaved since Saturday evening, and his beard was beginning to grow too much. His face itched, and he didn't like the feeling. He also didn't like that a company as large as Elliot Plastics would intentionally put little guys out of business. "They want to destroy me?"

She nodded. "Well, maybe not you, exactly. They want to ensure that they keep gaining market share for Christmas trees. They've bought up a few tree farms, and I'd bet that land is going to be repurposed next year for something else. Maybe they'll make products they need for other items they manufacture. I don't really know." Sadie rubbed the back of her neck. "I kinda didn't make it that long before I completely and totally went off on Wesley."

A deep rumble started low in his gut and when it started to make noise, Cody realized he was about to begin laughing. And not the ha-ha sort of laugh, but the kind that made a man bend over and clutch his stomach, followed by tears leaking from his eyes. "Wesley? An enemy? Isn't he just one of those rich, yacht sorta guys? What can he do?"

Sadie winced. "He's pretty powerful in the world of high finance and corporate America. If he decides to attack, I doubt we can counter him in time."

"Well, I'm not too worried. We've got the greatest warrior ever on our side." Cody wasn't oblivious to the danger of a man like Wesley, but he was confident that God had his back.

"Who?" Sadie asked.

"God." Only a week ago he wouldn't have said, or even thought that. Maybe Cody really was growing closer to his Savior.

Sadie was a believer, and she had shown she had faith in Cody, but at that moment, she looked like she wasn't so sure.

"Think about it. When God wanted to defeat any enemy of Israel's, he went first and took them down." Cody nodded, feeling more and more confident. "I'm not saying God is going to kill our enemies, but I do feel a sense of a peace right now."

Sadie's face flushed, then began to shine. "You might be right. We have God's protection."

"So, does this mean you're not leaving to head back to Seattle?" It sounded to Cody like Sadie wasn't going to get back with the dingleberry, but would she be able to take a job with a company who set out to destroy small businesses?

With brightened eyes, Sadie slowly shook her head. "I was never going to leave. I needed to hear Wesley out only because I know him. When he sets his mind to something, he's like a dog with a bone. He would have continued to hound me and not let up. So I listened. And asked questions."

"Wow, I'm surprised you're going to pass up an offer like that."

Sadie's head jerked back almost as though Cody had hit her. "You think I'd marry a guy that like? I thought you knew me better than that."

When Cody realized what he'd said, he was mortified. He put his hands in the air and waved them. "No, no. That's not what I meant. I meant I was surprised you'd pass up a chance at a real job in Seattle again. Wasn't that your plan when you arrived originally? To regroup and then head back to Seattle?"

Cody felt like an utter jerk when he noticed how Sadie's face fell.

She sighed. "It was what I wanted, before."

"And now?" Cody couldn't help but ask.

Sadie shrugged. "I don't really know. But nothing in that offer was what I wanted. I could never work for a company that treats people with such utter contempt. It sounds to me as though they're intentionally going to try and put an entire industry out of business. Or at the very least, chop it down until only a few trees are left."

Cody realized his hands were shaking and wiped the nervousness from them. While he wasn't a big-city guy, nor did he have a lot of business connections, he did know the difference between right and wrong. Usually it was the big-city guys who won battles against men like him. But God was telling him it was all going to be alright. He knew without a shadow of a doubt that he needed to put his trust in God.

And it was just like God to send an angel of mercy when he needed it most.

"Sadie, Cody, it's so good to see the both of you here together." Mrs. Claus grinned at them with a twinkle in her eyes as she looked at them both, and then to her husband.

"Mrs. Claus, Santa." Cody nodded to them. "It's nice to see you, too. But aren't you here a little early today? I thought you weren't going to visit until later tonight?" Cody had his own Santa, but a few times a week the one they all thought of as the real Santa would come out to visit with the kids and take pictures. His schedule was never announced so as to make it more of a treat than anything else. It also seemed like a challenge for the area families. They kept coming out, trying to get a glimpse of the real Santa.

"Ho, ho, ho. Mrs. Claus felt a pull to the farm today." Santa winked at his wife and put an arm around her shoulders.

"I'm sorry, but I couldn't help but overhear a little bit of your conversation. Is there really a company who wants to destroy Christmas? All for the sake of making more money?" Mrs. Claus tsk'd and pursed her lips.

Cody looked to Sadie and waited for her. It was her information, after all.

"Right," Sadie said when she read the question in Cody's eyes. Then she told the jolly couple what she had learned the previous night.

Santa rubbed his whiskers and "hmm'd" a lot before nodding, and then said, "Right. I got the feeling the other night that Wesley was on the naughty list as a kid."

Sadie laughed. She had always believed in their town Santa, but this was taking it a bit too far. "You didn't know him as a kid. You only deliver presents to the kids of Frenchtown, right?"

When Santa winked and put a white-gloved finger to the side of his nose, both Cody and Sadie weren't so sure they knew the *truth* about their Santa after all.

"Of course, dear." Mrs. Claus patted Sadie's shoulder and looked at her indulgently, then turned to her husband. "I think this is something we should look into further. We can't have naughty-list boys ruining Christmas for everyone else."

When Santa narrowed his eyes, Cody felt chills running down his spine. He had never seen Santa look angry before, not even during the year when the jolly man was known as Chris. If the look on Santa's face was anything to go by, some of those movies about not crossing Santa might have it right.

"You leave Wesley Watership to me. I'll take care of this." The fearful look morphed into his normal jovial face and the tension in the room vanished. "Now, why don't the two of you get to work? This place is about to open any minute now."

"Oh!" Sadie gasped. She looked down at her wristwatch. "I'm sorry, I totally lost track of time. Where's Daniel? I'll go help him."

Mrs. Claus interrupted before Cody could say anything. "He's off on a mission of his own, which is partly why I came to help. Why don't I see to the animals while you two walk the grounds?"

Cody had already walked the grounds and everything seemed ready to go, but he wasn't about to contradict Mrs. Claus. Especially not after seeing how scary Santa could be when one crossed him. "Alright Sadie, let's go." He took her hand and led her out.

As they left the barn, Cody overheard Santa and his wife talking. "I knew that Wesley was trouble from the moment I saw him in town last week."

"Yes, dear. You did mention him to me. But what about this Elliot Plastics?" Mrs. Claus's voice became too low to hear the farther away Cody walked, and he missed out on the rest of their conversation.

Sadie raised her brows. "Wow. Talk about a power couple."

When Cody's nose twitched, Sadie laughed, and Cody caught her bug and couldn't help letting a chuckle escape.

"You know, when you're around I seem to smile and laugh more than I have in years. Why is that?" Cody tilted his head and examined Sadie as they walked toward the small tree lot next to the barn full of beautiful trees already cut and just waiting for families to choose.

"I don't know," Sadie admitted. "Maybe you just needed someone to push you." Then she pushed him into a giant pile of snow that had been pressed aside by the snowplow that morning.

"Why you," Cody growled out, then reached up and pulled Sadie down next to him.

She screamed, but not from fright. Cody had pushed her down on her back next to him, and he hovered above her. As he looked intently into her eyes, she relaxed and put a hand up to his face. "Cody?"

"Hm?" The only thing Cody could see was the beautiful woman lying in the snow pile next to him. And all he wanted in that moment was to take her lips and make them his. He moved closer to her, but slowly so as to give her time to push him away or say no.

Nothing else in the world mattered in that very moment. Cody could feel the heartbeat of the woman he was coming to care for very much. When his lips were right over hers, he felt the heat of her gasps. Unsure if she wanted this or not, he stole his gaze from her lips up to her eyes. They were closed, and an angelic aura surrounded her head.

Cody knew right then and there that this was the woman for him, and she wanted his kiss. Hopefully she wanted it just as badly as he did. He looked back at her sweet lips before closing the rest of the distance between them.

At first his kiss was sweet and light, but as her lips moved with his, his kiss became more intense. He wrapped his arms around her back and pulled her closer to him, away from the snow bank.

Sadie wrapped her arms around his neck and returned his passion.

After all conscious thought left them both and they felt as though they were floating on air, a gruff voice broke into their moment of emotion. "Hey, this is a family establishment. The kids are waiting at the gate right now."

Cody pulled back quickly and looked up into his grandpops' toothless grin. All of a sudden he was sixteen again and getting caught by the same man, although that time grandpops had all of his teeth when he caught Cody kissing little Sarah Anderson in the hayloft of his barn. Though, to be fair, that kiss was tame compared to what he and Sadie had just shared.

Sadie stood up with pink covering her entire face. "Right. Of course." She coughed and turned away, straightening her jacket and then her hair.

Cody grinned.

Grandpops boxed his ears.

"Hey, what was that for?" Cody was now of age and could kiss whomever he darn well pleased.

"Don't be a dingleberry. Go after her," Grandpops gruffed.

When Cody stood up, he looked at his grandfather. "What have I said about walking about without your teeth?"

"Who's the adult here?" Joseph put his fisted hands on his hips and grinned.

Cody could help it, he chuckled and waved his grandfather back to the house. Then he turned and headed to find Sadie.

Chapter 25

S adie was so embarrassed. And also disappointed in herself. Kissing Cody was one thing, but *that* kiss? Oh, jingle bells. She was in over her head. Had she known cowboys kissed so well, she probably never would have left Montana.

Then she went and did the unpardonable: she compared Cody's kiss to Wesley's. Only in her mind, but still. A lady should never do such a thing, and she knew this. But, well, now she realized Wesley's kisses were more liked a codfish. That thought almost had her busting a gut, but then guilt kicked in.

However, as she walked she considered what Wesley was up to and decided the one lapse in thought was alright, but she never wanted to remember his kisses again.

"Sadie." Cody touched her arm, and she felt heat roiling through her entire being.

When she turned around, Sadie felt like her cheeks were on fire and couldn't bring herself to look at Cody. "Hi."

"I'm sorry for my grandpops." He stood before her, moving his weight from one foot to another. "And for kissing you like that in public."

Was he apologizing for the public display? She looked up into his warm, gray eyes and began to melt all over. It was a good thing she was no longer lying on that snow pile, for it would have most definitely melted if she had still been there.

He reached out for her hand, and she gave it to him. "How about we go out for dinner tonight? Nothing special, as I doubt we'll have time, but maybe we can go into town and share a meal at the diner?"

She noticed he was holding his breath, waiting for her reply. And when she agreed, a huge smile covered his face as Cody took a deep breath.

When they entered the diner, Dixie Hargrave, the diner's owner, grinned and led them to a table in the back. "It's good to see the both of you here, together." She winked at Cody and walked away after handing them their menus.

"What do you think she meant?" Sadie looked from Dixie's retreating form to Cody.

He grinned. "I think Dixie likes the idea of us being together. Or maybe she just wants to make sure you stay in town?"

Sadie tilted her head and sucked in her lower lip. "I think, everyone likes how much you've been smiling lately."

"Hey, what's that supposed to mean?"

"It means, Mr. Grinch..." Sadie winked. "That you used to be a young man who smiled. I've heard plenty of people commenting on how much you've changed recently." While Sadie wanted his change to be because of her, she also understood that something bad had happened fifteen years ago. More than just his parents death.

Cody sighed and put his menu down on the table in front of him. "Yeah, about that..."

Before Cody could say more, Lulu, Dixie's granddaughter and everyone's favorite waitress, walked up. She was sporting a poodle skirt, like something her hero, Sandy from the movie Grease, would have worn. When the bubble she had blown popped, she grinned and asked, "What can I get started for y'all?"

Sadie loved this girl. Lulu would be going away to culinary school soon, but Sadie hoped the girl would come back and take over the diner for her grandmother. She had a way of always knowing the best item on the menu for that day. "I'll have a diet coke and what do you suggest for dinner tonight?"

Lulu continued to chew her gum. She held her note pad in one hand and the pencil in the other. "I take it you two are in a hurry tonight?"

"How'd you know?" Cody asked.

"Because word's out that Santa's at your tree farm tonight." Lulu grinned. "And we all know what that means."

With a nod, Cody handed his menu to Lulu. "I'll take a hot cocoa and whatever you think is best."

"Right, two bowls of beef stew with fresh, hot sourdough bread coming right up." Lulu walked away after taking their menus.

"So, back to what I was about to ask." Sadie looked around before continuing, "what happened to make you turn into a Grinch?"

Cody sighed and ran a hand down his face. Then he looked around. "This is really not the best place for this conversation, but maybe we can start it here."

"And continue it on the drive back to your farm?" Sadie needed to know what happened to make him so untrusting of her and their fledgling relationship. When he ran out on her, it hurt. However, he had mentioned something the other day about this not being the first time a woman hurt him. There had to be a story and she needed to know what she was getting herself into.

They all had baggage. But the question really was, could he put the past where it belonged? And move forward?

After Lulu put their drinks on the table and walked away, Cody leaned forward. "You know about my parents dying in the blizzard, right?"

Sadie's heart ached for the pain Cody must have gone through as a young man. "Yes, you were away at college when your parent's car went off the road in a blizzard. They weren't found until later the next day…" she cleared her throat of the emotion she felt, "when it was too late."

His nostrils flared and Cody stared into his hot drink. "Yeah. But that's only part of my story."

Not wanting to push him, Sadie took a long drink of her Diet Coke and waited for him to continue. She noticed Cody sniffed and rubbed one of his eyes. Probably trying to keep any tears forming at bay.

"I was dating a woman at college, Mary Beth. I really thought I was going to marry her." Cody stopped when he noticed Chloe and Brandon coming their way.

Brandon held up a hand in greeting. "Cody, Sadie, how's it going?"

Dixie sat the two of them in the booth right next to Cody and Sadie, effectively postponing their conversation.

"Good, good. Very busy." Cody waved at the couple but didn't smile.

Sadie, however, stood up and went to Chloe to hug her. "Chloe, you must be getting excited for the big day?" Chloe and Brandon were planning a wedding and the entire town was excited for the couple.

"We are. I tell you, we should have eloped. This big wedding stuff is nuts. And it's taking all of my time and energy." Chloe sat down and turned to look at Sadie.

Sadie couldn't help but laugh. "That's what all brides say. Then when the big day arrives, they always say it was well worth the hassles."

Lulu showed up with Sadie and Cody's beef stew. Then took the order for Chloe and Brandon.

The four of them chatted across the booths while Sadie and Cody ate their stew.

The moment Sadie finished hers, she pushed the bowl away from her. "Cody, are you ready? I think we should head back as soon as possible. The tree farm is going to be crazy by now."

He nodded.

"I heard about Santa visiting your farm tonight. Good luck." Chloe waved and they all said their goodbyes.

Cody took the check and led Sadie to the front where he paid the bill and handed Lulu a generous tip.

Sadie noticed what Cody had done and felt pride well up. While the town did help local high school students with small scholarships, it didn't include those going to trade schools, or culinary school. Lulu needed all of the help she could get to pay her way.

For a man who had been known as the town Grinch for at least the past decade, Cody had really changed lately. He was turning into the opposite of Grinch. So when Cody looked at her and frowned, Sadie wondered what was going through his head.

The moment they were in his truck and on the road back to the farm, Sadie turned to look at him. "Cody, what's wrong?"

"Nothing." He looked straight ahead. "Well, I was thinking about Mary Beth and how I did need to talk to you about all of this."

Sadie sat up straight in her seat and gulped. "Whatever you want to tell me, I'm here for you."

"When my parents died, I came home. At first I wasn't sure that I'd have to quite college so I told Mary Beth to stay there. Not that she had offered to come with me. I should have known when she looked at me funny." He snorted and shook his head. "Actually, I should have known sooner."

"What do you mean?"

"You know how when you're in the middle of a relationship that's heading for disaster, but you don't know it? Things seem like they're fine. Sure, weird stuff happens, but you always come up with some sort of excuse or other for why your partner has pulled away. Or why she's cancelled several dates at the last minute."

While Sadie hadn't dated much in college, she did understand. Things with Wesley had been similar before she lost her job. "Then when you look back on everything, it hits you. All the signs you missed of something else going on."

"Exactly." Cody pointed to Sadie. "I should have seen it coming but I was so in love." He shook his head. "Or I thought I was in love. Instead, I was just oblivious and only saw what I wanted to see."

"Yeah, it was just easier to think stress was getting to him. Work deadlines got in the way of a few dates. That sort of thing? Or I guess in your case, college workload and tests?" Sadie looked to Cody for confirmation.

He nodded. "Yeah. We had been growing apart but I ignored the signs." He waved a hand. "Anyway, turns out she was dating someone else the last few weeks I was in college and I never knew it."

"Which caused your trust issues. And when Wesley showed up, you thought I had done the same?" It was all coming together for Sadie now. While it didn't excuse Cody for leaving without talking to her first, she could understand.

"Yup. And when I finally got my head back on straight, it had to have been almost two months after my parents died, I went to see her."

"Let me guess, she was in the arms of this other guy when you saw her?" That would cause Sadie to be mistrustful of men, too. Especially if she was trying to deal with everything Cody was at that time. It couldn't have been easy to bury both of his parents and discover that it was up to him to take over the tree farm.

"No, worse."

Sadie frowned. "How so?"

"I went to her dorm room and when she answered, she had on this huge rock of an engagement ring. She flaunted it about before she told me she was marrying Handley Hamilton the Third."

"Ouch." Sadie didn't understand those type of girls. Mary Beth had been dating Cody, one the nicest guys she'd ever met. And while he was dealing with the death of his parents, she was messing around with another guy, and didn't even have the guts to tell him. "I take it you didn't have much contact with her right after you left school?"

Cody shook his head. "I called a couple of times and left her messages, she left me a few messages. But we only spoke like once or twice. There always seemed to be so much going on."

"So, not only were you mad at God for taking your parents, but you were mad at Him for taking the one girl you thought you loved at the same exact time." She didn't need to ask, she knew that's what had caused Cody's issues with God and women.

"That about sums it up." Cody winced and turned down the road that led to his tree farm. There was a long line of vehicles down the road waiting to park. "Wow."

"Yeah. Maybe we shouldn't have gone into town for dinner tonight?" Sadie looked around at all of the people. It was a good thing they had set aside a few parking spots out front of Cody's house for them, or they'd be at least another hour trying to find parking and then catching a ride on one of the wagons taking people in and out.

"No, I think we needed the time away to talk." Cody looked at her and grinned.

"Okay, maybe we did. But, I think until things slow down, we should eat here." Sadie arched a brow, just daring him to disagree.

Cody held up one hand, while the other stayed on the steering wheel. "I won't object. The food we sell here is pretty good." He grinned at her when he had to stop to let a family cross the road.

"And now? How are you feeling about God and everything that happened?" Sadie knew he had grown a lot with his relationship with God over the past few weeks. She had seen it. He spoke more about his Lord and Savior the past two weeks than he had before that. Plus, he seemed to genuinely enjoy the church services lately. She had seen him and watched how he followed along in his Bible and kept his attention on the pastor. The first time she noticed him in church, he did more looking around at everyone else then he did the pastor.

Cody focused on getting through the crowds safely. Once he was parked, he turned off his truck and turned in his seat to look at her. "I think I've come a long way over the past two months. I know I'll always have new things to learn, and trusting in God's plan is something I might not always get right, but I know He has the entire story in front of Him. He knows exactly how it all ends." He rubbed a hand down his face.

"Cody, I think that's something we all struggle with at times. Especially lately. So much evil has entered this world. So many good people are hurt and die young while the worst of the worst always seem to come out ahead." He wasn't the only one who struggled with these issues. Sadie had done the same when she first lost her job and then her boyfriend.

"I know. Life's not fair. But sin had consequences that we can't always understand." Cody looked behind Sadie.

She turned. "Yeah, we should probably get going and help out where we can."

He took her hand. "But, as long as we remember that God is in control, and everything is part of His ultimate plan, I think we can get through this."

"And we have to always stay in prayer and read our Bible," Sadie added.

Cody snorted. "Yes, reading the Bible daily is key."

She nodded and took her seatbelt off. "And always go to God in prayer."

Cody got out of the truck and came over to open the door for Sadie. Then they headed back to where all of the people lined up to see Santa and Mrs. Claus.

Santa noticed Cody and Sadie walking hand in hand as they came back from dinner. He motioned to the couple when he caught his wife's attention.

Mrs. Claus smiled and said to no one in particular, "I think they're going to be very happy together." Then she turned back to the ladies who had lined up to buy copies of the calendar featuring the men of Frenchtown.

When it began to snow, Jessica looked back to her husband and smiled. The both of them loved a good snow, and this year they had received so much snow that the Christmas festivities around town, and there at the tree farm, carried an extra-special dose of Christmas magic.

"Now, if only I could get Megan and Daniel together."

Chapter 26

"**S**adie, come here," Lottie called out as her friend entered the Frenchtown Roasting Company. There were only three days left until Christmas, and everyone had been running around like chickens with their heads cut off.

"Hi, Lottie. Let me place my order and then I'll come and sit with you." Sadie waved and got in line. It seemed she wasn't the only person who needed a little extra caffeine and sugar to get through the last few days before Christmas.

"Whew, that was a long line. Has it been like this all day?" Sadie asked when she sat at the table with Lottie.

The proprietress nodded. "Yes, it's been crazy ever since the booths at the tree farm emptied. Now everyone is coming to town to get their last-minute trees and stopping in here for coffee."

"Don't forget your wonderful Christmas pastries. I must say, one of your gingerbread cookies along with the gingerbread latte is the best treat. I hate that they won't be around come the new year." Sadie pouted and hoped Lottie would keep her favorite treats on the menu a while longer.

Lottie patted her friend's hand. "I'll keep serving gingerbread lattes just as long as we have the syrup. Once it runs out, that's it." She shrugged. "But that's not what I wanted to talk to you about." A mischievous grin crossed her face before she replaced it with a mask of cool indifference.

"Uh-oh, I know that look." Sadie pointed to her friend's face and waited.

Quinn Keith, Lottie's darling little girl, came running over to the table. "Did you show her?"

"Show me what?" Sadie asked as she hugged the little nine-year-old girl.

"Momma made a special gift for my new daddy." Lottie had recently married Cove Hamilton, one of the men from the calendar, and Quinn was going all over town making sure everyone knew she finally had a dad. Her dad died when she was just a baby, and she didn't remember him. She could only remember Cove when he came to visit her on his few days off each year.

Sadie turned to Lottie and arched a brow. "Special gift?" It was too soon to think that Lottie might be pregnant, but it wasn't impossible. Was that what Quinn meant by "making a special gift?" Had Lottie called the baby a bun in the oven? She grinned.

"Oh, no. I know what that look means. And definitely not." It was Lottie's turn to point a finger. "It has to do with the calendar."

With her elbow on the table, Sadie put her chin in her hand and waited for Lottie to explain.

Lottie looked around and giggled. Then pulled up a tote bag from under the table. "Now, this has to stay a secret. I don't want Cove to see it until Christmas morning."

"Alright, I doubt I'll see him anyway." Sadie shrugged.

"That means no telling anyone else, either. Especially Cody." Lottie looked pointedly at Sadie.

She raised both palms. "Alright, alright. My lips are sealed." Then she made the motion of closing a zipper over her mouth.

Lottie unzipped the top of the tote bag and pulled out a gift that had already been wrapped.

Sadie frowned. "Um…" She scratched her head. It didn't look like a calendar. It looked like a shirt box. She supposed Lottie could have put a calendar in the box and wrapped it.

Lottie stared at her, waiting for Sadie to see it. She waggled the gift in front of Sadie's face.

Then Sadie turned her attention to the wrapping paper and covered her mouth before the squeal could escape. "Where in the world did you get that made?"

"Turns out there are quite a few places online where you can have custom wrapping paper made from pictures. I chose a Christmas red background with snowflakes, and they added the ten photos I sent them." Lottie giggled, joined by her little girl.

"Daddy is going to love this, isn't he?" Quinn turned her sweet, innocent smile up at Sadie.

Sadie didn't have the heart to tell the little girl that Cove would be so embarrassed if anyone saw this paper. Lottie had taken ten of the best pictures from the calendar shoot and used them. One of the pictures on the wrapped present was of all twelve men, but the rest were strictly of Cove in different poses.

But what would have embarrassed the poor cowboy was the fact that the picture sitting right on top, where a bow should be, was the one of him falling off the bull.

When they did the photoshoot all those weeks ago, they decided to get an old bull so as not to hurt Cove or cause any great ruckus. The bull didn't take too kindly to Cove sitting on him, at first. And they were able to get some great motion shots of Cove riding a bull. It was one of those that they'd used for the calendar.

But this picture. Sadie had to keep her hand over her mouth while she kept giggling.

Lottie put the box back in the bag and zipped it up.

When Cove saw this, Sadie knew he'd want the negative destroyed.

That old bull had bucked him but good. You could tell from the look of utter shock and dismay on his face that Cove did not expect an old bull to buck him, one of the best bull riders in recent history, off its back.

"So, do you have any extra paper? And where can I get some made?" This was too good of an opportunity to pass up. Sadie was going to have to get her own rolls made of Cody. Now he didn't have any truly embarrassing pictures, but there were a few funny faces made at the beginning of the photoshoot.

Quinn nodded. "We got enough to wrap his presents for years. Don't we, Mommy?" The little girl looked her mom.

Lottie patted her daughter on the head. "We sure do, little Queenie."

When Sadie left the coffee shop, she was planning on checking out that website and placing her order that very day. It was too late to get a roll in time for this Christmas, but Cody's birthday was coming up soon.

Speaking of the handsome cowboy...there he was standing tall and too good looking to miss.

"Well, howdy, Sadie." Cody stood just outside the Frenchtown Roasting door. Which caused Sadie to stop right in the middle of the exit.

"Hey, cowboy. What brings you to town?" Sadie leaned up against the door post and grinned at her man.

When Codie looked up, his face glowed with anticipation.

Sadie looked up and felt the heat rushing to her cheeks. "Really, right here? What was Lottie thinking?"

Cody sidled up closer to Sadie and took her by her hips and pulled her close. "I think she was thinking that some of us cowboys needed a little prodding."

She wrapped her arms around his neck. "Hmm, mmm. But not this cowboy, right?"

He shook his head. "No ma'am."

His smoldering eyes turned to her lips and Sadie felt her mouth go dry and she had to lick her lips. Above them was one of the mistletoe boughs Cody sold at his tree farm. All this time and Sadie hadn't noticed it hanging up there above the entrance. How could she have missed it?

Cody didn't waste any time in taking her lips with his. Sadie felt the passion, but also the restraint in his embrace. Cody's lips moved, and Sadie's perfectly countered as though they had been doing this dance all their lives.

When they finally parted, it was to a round of raucous applause, hoots, and hollers.

Someone in the crowd called out, "nice mistletoe kiss."

Another one asked, "is this why you sell so much mistletoe?"

And another said, "where can I get me some of those mistletoe kisses?"

Sadie put her forehead on Cody's shoulders and could have died of embarrassment as way too many townsfolks watched them kiss. "Stupid parasite. All it does is get people in trouble."

Cody chuckled and hugged her tighter. "Oh, I don't know about that." Then he looked up and grinned. "I'd say it's a romantic parasite."

Epilogue

T he Christmas season went quite well. While there might have been a few glitches, Sadie and Cody worked them out together. With a bit of help in the background from Santa and Mrs. Claus.

The threat of bankruptcy went away, and Cody's tree farm had done so well that the local news continued to send reporters out on a regular basis. Which in turn kept the attention on them and brought more visitors from as far away as Idaho, Wyoming, and Colorado.

"So, Mr. Money Bags, what are you going to do now?" Sadie hugged her cowboy and looked up into his eyes.

Cody wrapped his precious cowgirl in his arms as they stood on the back porch of his farmhouse watching the snow come down, layering the already thick carpet with more soft flakes. "I think I'm going to work with the town council to ensure that between the town and my Christmas tree farm, we have enough coverage next year to handle all of the visitors."

Sadie nodded. "Yeah, some of the town events were overshadowed by us, weren't they?" While she loved that Cody had done so well, she hated that a few of the events in town didn't do as much business as normal, and she knew that was because they hadn't planned this year the way they should have.

"I also want to get a pumpkin patch going and try to bring people in early. Maybe get more booths created this spring and summer so we can have a real fall festival out here." Cody kissed the top of Sadie's head.

Grandpops came outside with a huge grin and his teeth in. "Did you see the news?"

Cody and Sadie turned around with confused looks on their faces.

"Which news, Grandpops?" Cody asked.

The old man pointed to Sadie. "About your ex-dingleberry." He cackled and waved them inside. "It's cold out there, come on in and have some of my hot apple cider. I'm trying out a new recipe for the fall festival Cody and I are gonna host next year."

In the background, the song "Baby It's Cold Outside" was playing softly, and the TV was turned off.

"I heard about that. But Joseph, tell me about Wesley. What's going on?" Sadie hadn't spoken one word to the man since she went off on him after he ruined her community Thanksgiving dinner last month. She also hadn't heard anything from Blue Sky Marketing. The only time she'd thought about Wesley had been two weeks after he left town. She wondered if the job offer was real, or if it was one of Wesley's stupid scams. Then when she realized she didn't care, she put him and the job out of her mind.

"It seems your guy…" Joseph began, but was cut off by Sadie.

"He hasn't been my guy for almost a year now." Sadie glared at Joseph, not wanting anyone to associate Wesley Watership with her ever again.

Joseph coughed. "Well, he's in a lot of hot water over some scam he was running. Did you know he was working a pyramid scheme on his clients?" Joseph handed her a cup of his new hot apple cider that also had a tad bit of nutmeg and cinnamon.

"Really? Wesley?" Sadie's nose scrunched and she looked to Cody.

Both of them looked back at Joseph and waited for him to explain.

"I don't know all the details, but he was robbing Peter to pay Paul, and taking a huge cut." Joseph pointed to Sadie. "That company he said wanted to hire you, they're the ones who reported his misdeeds to the po-po. It's a good thing you never went back with him. You might have been implicated in his schemes."

Sadie's face went white, and she stumbled to a chair. "Are you sure?"

"Just as sure as I am that the sun will rise tomorrow." Joseph's brows furrowed, and he watched Sadie. "Are you alright?"

She nodded. "Yeah, I'm just shocked. All this time I thought he was a good guy. A bit misguided in business at times, but good."

"Just goes to show you can't always trust city slickers." Joseph tsk'd and took a sip of his hot cider.

Cody rubbed Sadie's back. "Did you have any idea?"

She shook her head. "None at all."

"Well, good riddance, I say." Grandpops nodded and grinned.

"I think we should look to the future, and not the past. In two days' time it will be New Year's Eve, and then a brand new year will be upon us." Cody turned to Sadie and took both of her hands in his. "Sadie McKinley, will you be my date for the New Year's Eve dance at the Cattleman's Association?"

"Yes, I'd love to be your date, Cody Makinaw." Sadie had eyes only for Cody, and when she began to slowly move closer to him with the idea of kissing him, Grandpops coughed loudly.

"Hey now, none of that funny business. You two aren't married. So keep it PG." Grandpops laughed and then faked a choking noise.

"Not yet, but soon." Cody leaned down and placed a chaste kiss on Sadie's cheek and prayed that when he did propose, the woman he was falling in love with would accept.

Cody and Sadie's story has come to it's happily ever after conclusion. But don't miss out on Her Sleigh Ride Christmas Cowboy, the story of Megan and Daniel!

Keep going for a sneak peek!

And don't miss out on this yummy, and super easy, pumpkin-chip croissant!

Sadie's Pumpkin-chip Croissant a la mode

1 package frozen puff pastry sheet

Orange flavored cooking chips. (usually I get these from Micheal's in their baking section.)

Pumpkin spice flavored cooking chips. (same as above)

Vanilla bean ice cream

Optional: mini choc chips

Topping:

You can use either cinnamon sugar or colored cupcake toppings from the baking section of your local grocery store, or Micheal's. You can also melt the flavored chips and drizzle them over the finished pastries. I tend to do a mixture so I have a pretty display.

Follow the directions on the package for the puff pastry sheets. These are normally found in your grocer's freezer and should be kept frozen until right before you make this.

Set oven to 375 (or whatever the pastry package says)

Take a cookie sheet and cover it with parchment paper. (this keeps the pastries from sticking to the sheet when they are done)

Put out a sheet of parchment paper on your counter. Roll out the puff pastry dough on the sheet. Using a pizza cutter, cut the size and shapes you want. I usually do triangles, like when making pigs in a blanket.

From the larger end, place in the chips you choose to use. I mix the flavors but go a little heavier on the pumpkin spice. You can also add in some mini chocolate chips if you only want a small taste of fall.

Roll the dough, while keeping the chips inside, until you have the pointed end on the top. Pinch it just a tiny bit to ensure it stays while baking.

Put the pan in the oven. Start with 8 minutes. Check the pastry and see if the chips are melted and the puff pastry is lightly browned. Keep adding another minute or two until you have the right look.

Pull it out right away. If using cinnamon sugar, sprinkle that on right away while the pastry is hot. If using the drizzle method with melted chocolate, wait until the pasty has cooled thoroughly (usually a 3 hrs), then drizzle on top. You can also put in the fridge for at least 40 minutes to cool down, but only do this if you're in a hurry.

With the cinnamon sugar topping, it's very nice to warm up and eat with your morning, or afternoon, coffee. Or PSL (See Her Sleigh Ride Christmas Cowboy for the PSL recipe.)

With the drizzle on top, you can still warm up the pastry, but be careful you don't overheat it, the drizzle might melt off.

And never forget to top off a treat like this with a scoop of vanilla bean ice cream!

I will be posting pictures in my newsletter, so subscribe to see how mine came out. And enjoy your fall treat!

Author's Notes

T hank you so much for picking up my book and reading it. I couldn't keep doing this if it weren't for people like you! I really do appreciate everyone who reads my books and am truly grateful for those who recommend it to friends or leave reviews. Word of mouth is the best way to discover new books!

There is one more book to this series, and then it will be completed. So be sure to grab your copy of Her Sleigh Ride Christmas Cowboy!

Next year (2022), I'll be starting a new Cowboy Christmas series, so keep an eye out.

I wanted to give a huge shout out to the readers and fans who have messaged me this past year after reading Her Montana Christmas Cowboy! Thank you so much for your notes of encouragement. Some of you are from Montana and you noted how well I set the stage for this series. While the Frenchtown in my book is based upon the real Frenchtown, Montana, my town is a bit bigger and set up differently.

Last summer I drove through Montana, checking out various locations to set my books, and Frenchtown was basically a gas station, bank, and a few shop fronts. I'm sure there was more, but that was all that was directly off the interstate. And of course, there were a lot of ranches and farms around the area. It was the ranches and farms that caught my attention.

It also seemed the perfect location for a Christmas Tree Farm! Right off the interstate, and in an area of the state that already had plenty of evergreen trees and beautiful view of the mountains and prairies. If you ever get the chance to visit Montana, do it! And don't miss out on seeing Glacier National Park.

Speaking of which, keep an out later next year for a brand-new series that's close to Glacier!

Keep reading for that sneak peek I promised.

May God Bless you this Christmas, and through the year!

Jenna

Let's Keep In Touch

For those of you who love social media, here are the various ways to follow or contact me:

BookBub: https://www.bookbub.com/authors/jenna-hendricks

Instagram: https://www.instagram.com/j.l.hendricks/

Twitter: https://twitter.com/TinkFan25

Facebook: https://www.facebook.com/people/JL-Hendricks/100011419945971

Website: https://jennahendricks.com

Newsletter Sign-up

Do you love clean & wholesome contemporary cowboy romance? Want more? Then check out Finding Love in Montana today!

By signing up for my newsletter, you'll not only receive this book, but a couple more free stories as well!

If you want to make sure you hear about the latest and greatest, sign up for my newsletter at: Subscribe to Jenna Hendricks newsletter. I will only send out a few e-mails a month. I'll do cover reveals, snippets of new books, and giveaways or promos in the newsletter, some of which will only be available to newsletter subscribers. (https://jennahendricks.com/newsletter/)

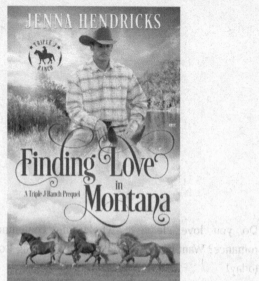

Sneak Peek

W hen Daniel met Megan, he made an utter fool of himself. Can he turn things around in time for a Merry Christmas with the beautiful cowgirl?

Daniel is the Big Sky Christmas Tree Farm's foreman. He's never been good with women. Seriously, he has foot in mouth disease. Whenever a pretty woman is around, he says the stupidest things the moment his mouth opens. It's almost as if his mouth is trying to ruin any chance at all with a pretty cowgirl. Normally, it doesn't bother him that women ignore him.

But Megan's Different.

Now, Daniel wants to say the right things, and get a date with the pretty counselor from the Crooked Arrow Ranch.

Megan Anderson is a tough, no nonsense Army veteran who has seen her share of awful. Now she's working at a ranch designed to help the wounded heroes get the emotional support they need in order to ease back into civilian life. It's not easy coming home broken.

Sometimes, those cracks in a soldier's armor aren't always physical, but mental. And it's her job to help mend them. But this Daniel character is like no other man she's met. For one, he's never served his country a day in his life. And two, the strangest things come out of his mouth. When she sees how hard he's working to save the tree farm, Megan gives him a second look.

And that sleigh ride? Boy howdy! The twinkle in his eye is enough to get her to look past the proverbial boot in his mouth.

Will Megan figure out what's causing Daniel to be so rude? Or will she spend another Christmas all alone?

Come ride the Christmas sleigh through the tree farm one last time and see if true love will win out with a Christmas miracle.

Grab your copy today of Her Sleigh Ride Christmas Cowboy and see what happens when Daniel tries to help Megan and her mother.

CPSIA information can be obtained
at www.ICGtesting.com
Printed in the USA
LVHW090404181022
730945LV00005B/496